EXEGETICAL ESSAYS

ON

SEVERAL WORDS

RELATING TO

FUTURE PUNISHMENT.

BY MOSES STUART,
Professor of Sacred Literature in the Theol. Sem. at Andover.

Wipf and Stock Publishers
EUGENE, OREGON

Wipf and Stock Publishers
199 West 8th Avenue, Suite 3
Eugene, Oregon 97401

Exegetical Essays on Several Words Relating to Future Punishment
By Stuart, Moses
ISBN: 1-57910-898-9
Publication date: March, 2002
Previously published by Allen, Morrill and Wardwell, Andover, 1830.

PREFACE.

As no subject can be presented to the human mind so deeply interesting as the inquiry, whether we shall be happy or miserable in a future world through endless ages; so no apology is needed, for choosing such a topic of discussion in the following pages. Very many embrace the opinion, that the present is not our only state of probation; and of course, that if our lot be that of punishment in a future world, yet our condition even then is not to be regarded as hopeless. Has this any foundation in the Word of God, or does it proceed rather from our *wishes* than from reason and evidence?

The following pages do not profess to treat of these questions at large. It would require a volume of much greater size than the present, to do even tolerable justice to the whole subject. My design, however, is to discuss, almost entirely in a philological way, some of the most interesting topics relative to future punishment. This I have endeavoured to do, unembarrassed by any particular opinions or systems. My conscience bears me testimony, that I have endeavoured to come at my subject, in the way of an original and disinterested inquirer. If I have not always succeeded in doing this, I must beg the reader to attribute it to human infirmity, and not to design.

That I have not referred, in the general course of discussion, to those who differ from me in opinion, (one instance only excepted), they must not put to the score of neglect; for neither have I referred to those with whom I agree. My wish is, not to appear in a polemic attitude, on the one hand; nor in that of one who appeals for support to mere human authority, on the other. I hope this will not be considered as betraying any neglect of my opponents, or overlooking of those with whom I agree. Simple, philological disquisition, conducted by approved rules of interpretation, and unembarrassed by friend or foe to my own views, is what I have aimed at. How far I have succeeded, must be left, of course, to the judgement of my readers.

PREFACE.

One thing I do earnestly desire to say to the reader with affection and deep concern; 'Look well to it how thou examinest and judgest; it is for thy life!' If it were a matter of taste, or of common lexicographal or grammatical dispute, it would be of little consequence to give such an admonition; for the consequences could not be very important. But it is not so here; for the *interests of eternity* may be connected with the decision which the reader will make. As a philologist, I am unable to doubt the certainty of the conclusions to which the examination that is detailed in the following sheets has led me. Deeply impressed with this myself, it is natural that I should wish to impress others in like manner. If they do not agree with me, after examining the subject, they will not, I trust, take umbrage at the manner in which it has been brought before them.

In regard to the writer in the Christian Examiner, whose sentiments are briefly reviewed in p. 72 seq., my only apology for departing from the general rule which I have observed, and making opposition to him, is the earnest solicitation of some respected friends that I should take this course. I would rather have avoided it; but since I have done it, and the writer has replied in the Christian Examiner for Sept. 1830, I feel it to be my duty still farther to notice his reply; which I have done in a brief Appendix at the end of this little volume.

As my object is discussion on original and fundamental grounds, which have respect to the Hebrew and Greek Scriptures, so it must follow, that my book can be read intelligibly throughout, only by such as have some knowledge of these languages. Yet I have endeavoured so to write, that intelligent readers, unacquainted with Hebrew and Greek, may get at the scope of my arguments; and I would fain hope that in this I have succeeded.

I only add, that the time seems to have come, when appeal to the original Scriptures appears to be the only effectual method of satisfying the public mind, in regard to any controverted religious subject. That there is a portion of the public who will not be satisfied even with this, I deeply regret, but am constrained to believe. Yet since far the greater part profess to believe in the declarations of the Bible, to this I have made the appeal; and by this only I desire the doctrine in question, and my little treatise respecting it, to be tried.

M. STUART.

Andover, Oct. 1830.

ΑΙΩΝ and *ΑΙΩΝΙΟΣ*.

§ 1. *Importance of the subject.*

To a being endowed with a spirit which can never cease to exist, and who can live at most but a few years in the present world, the question, What is to be his *future* condition? is the most important question that can possibly be agitated. Will his condition after death be unchangeable? Will his probation be at an end, when his present life shall cease? And if so, on what does the happiness or misery of his future state depend?

An instinctive desire of happiness and dread of misery, form an elementary part of the nature which man possesses. They are interwoven with the very being of his soul, and must be immortal as the spirit from which they spring. At the prospect of happiness, he is filled with delightful anticipations, which make existence a blessing, and cause the soul to exult in the possession of its powers and capacities; at the prospect of misery without relief and without end, an instinctive horror closes every avenue of pleasure, and the soul loathes its own existence, and would fain resign the possession of it.

This, however, it cannot do. He who made us *in his own image*, made us immortal like himself; immortal in regard to the powers and faculties, as well as the existence, of the soul; the immortal subjects, therefore, of

§ 1. *Αἰών and Αἰώνιος.*

happiness or misery in the future state. We can no more cease to be the subjects of the one or the other, than we can cease to be what we are—rational, sentient beings, whose very constitution, whose essential nature, necessarily involves with its existence the experience of either happiness or misery.

However discrepant the views of men may be, in some respects, with regard to our condition in a future state, there will be—there can be—no important difference of opinion in regard to the point now under consideration; at least, there can be no important difference, among those who believe in the immortality of the soul. To all such, then, the questions, Whether we shall be happy or miserable in another world? and, Whether we shall be *unchangeably* so? are of such unspeakable moment, as to make all other questions appear to be of comparatively small importance.

How are these great questions to be answered? The immortal soul, that is not sunk in the grossest ignorance, or rendered insensible by the most debasing sensuality and love of the world, cannot but feel an interest—an all-pervading interest—in this inquiry. Good men exhibit their interest in it, by long-continued and solicitous inquiries into their spiritual condition and prospects; and even the wicked, in most cases, exhibit their interest also in the question, by their constant efforts, in one way and another, to bring themselves into a condition of quiet with regard to it.

All sober and rational men will surely be disposed to ask, From what quarter can these all-important inquiries have light thrown upon them? What cheering sun is there, which will shed his radiance over the darkness that rests upon them, and disclose the object of them to us by the full light of day?

§ 1. *Αἰών* and *Αἰώνιος*.

And is not the answer to these last inquiries comparatively easy? *The light of nature can never scatter the darkness in question.* This light has never yet sufficed to make even the question clear, to any portion of our benighted race, Whether the soul of man is immortal? Cicero, incomparably the most able defender of the soul's immortality of which the heathen world can yet boast, very ingenuously confesses, that after all the arguments which he had adduced in order to confirm the doctrine in question, it so fell out, that his mind was satisfied of it, only when directly employed in contemplating the arguments adduced in its favor. At all other times, he fell unconsciously into a state of doubt and darkness.

It is notorious, also, that Socrates, the next most able advocate among the heathen for the same doctrine, has adduced arguments to establish the never-ceasing existence of the soul, which will not bear the test of examination. Such is the argument by which he endeavors to prove, that we shall always continue to exist because we always have existed; and this last proposition he labors to establish, on the ground that all our present acquisitions of knowledge are only so many *reminiscences* of what we formerly knew, in a state of existence *antecedent* to our present one. Unhappy lot of philosophy, to be doomed thus to prop itself up, with supports so weak and fragile as this! How can the soul be filled with consolation, in prospect of death, without some better and more cheering light than can spring from such a source? How can it quench its thirst for immortality, by drinking in such impure and turbid streams as these? Poor wandering heathen! How true it is—and what a glorious, blessed truth it is—that " life and immortality are brought to light in the gospel !" It is equally true, that they are brought to light *only* there.

§ 1. *Αἰών and Αἰώνιος*.

Thus much then, is certainly plain. If the heathen did not, and (all their circumstances and passions considered) could not, sufficiently answer the inquiry which respects the immortal existence of the soul; much less could they *satisfactorily* answer the question, Whether our future state is to be happy or miserable? And if either, On what conditions is our happiness or misery suspended? These awfully momentous questions, they never did answer. 'The world by wisdom knew not God.' Nor did they know that he had made man in his own image; much less that man had been redeemed by the death of God's own beloved Son. They did not know any thing definite, respecting either the happiness which the gospel proffers to the penitent and obedient, or the miseries which are threatened to the impenitent and disobedient, in the world to come.

Nor has all the light which has been cast upon the subject of the soul's immortality, since the gospel was first published, enabled men, independently of the gospel itself, to demonstrate this truth; certainly not to shew, with any good degree of satisfaction, what the future state of the soul will be.

If there be any satisfactory light, then, on the momentous question of a future state, it must be sought from the word of God. After all the toil and pains of casuists and philosophers, it remains true, that the gospel, and the gospel only, has 'brought life and immortality to light' in a satisfactory manner.

Most men among us either expressly acknowledge this, or else implicitly concede it. The latter even those do, who make strenuous efforts to shew that the Scriptures can be construed in such a way, as to render the doctrine of the ultimate, universal happiness of mankind at least

§ 1. *Αἰών and Αἰώνιος.*

probable; although, at the same time, unconsciously perhaps to themselves, they reason from principles which are not deduced from the Scriptures, but from their own apprehensions in regard to what is proper or improper under the divine government of rational beings.

The Bible, then, is the only *sure* source of knowledge, in regard to the future destiny of our race. This alone is to be relied on, in the ultimate settlement of the great question, whether we are to be forever happy or miserable.

But how is this question to be settled by the Bible? Is this to be done, by carrying along with us, when we go to interpret the Bible, principles which decide beforehand what in our view the Bible *ought to speak*, and to draw from these, conclusions as to what it *does speak?* Is any other book on earth interpreted in this manner? Or at least if it be so, do not all men declaim against the unfairness and the partiality of such an interpretation? After all, surely it cannot be for the ultimate interest of any intelligent and rational being, who is favored with the Scriptures, to force on them a method of interpretation which he would complain of, when applied to any other book. It cannot be for his ultimate interest, to make a mistake in respect to the tremendous subject of a future state. Above all, if it should at last prove to be true, that the present life is the only state of probation for men, a mistake as to the consequences of this probation, must be of an importance which no language can describe, and of which no heart can even conceive.

And even supposing that there is a future state of probation, which is disciplinary, and in which the wicked are subjected to pain and distress; what reasonable and considerate man would desire to incur the risk of this, by

§ 1. *Αἰών* and *Αἰώνιος*.

flattering himself in such a way as to continue in his sinful course while in the present world, and venture upon the consequences of this in the world to come?

May it not be hoped, then, amid the conflicting spirit of the times, and the widely spread belief that all our race will eventually be happy in another world, that there are some, at least, who will feel it to be their duty and their interest, seriously and impartially to examine and consider what the Scriptures have said, relative to the important question about the *duration* of future happiness and misery? I must hope that there are at least some, (who have as yet been wandering in uncertainty, and who may have inclined, or rather have wished, to believe that they shall be finally happy, and that the Bible has not decided the question against the ultimate hopes of those that die in a state of impenitency), who will now consent seriously and carefully to examine the ground of their hopes and wishes, and to be guided by the sentiments of the Bible, investigated by means of the usual and impartial principles of interpretation.

For such, the following investigation is specially intended. It is not my design to occupy the *whole* ground, covered by the great question which relates to the inquiry, Whether our condition in a future world is immutable? To do this, would require a volume instead of a few pages. It would so multiply topics of consideration, also, as to have a tendency rather to distract and confuse the mind, than to enlighten and satisfy it in the most simple way.

I purposely avoid, therefore, all remarks here on objections against the doctrine of endless future punishment, drawn from considerations respecting the divine benevolence, which the minds of many men appear to entertain, in consequence of reasoning abstractedly and independently of the Scriptures about the nature of God and the desert of sin. To settle the question whether *endless* punishment is possible, *before* we come to the Scriptures for investigation; and then to search them merely to see whether we cannot find something to confirm our views, or to remove the difficulties which the Bible throws in our way; is virtually to renounce the Scriptures as our guide, and to set up our own conclusions and reasonings in the place of them. But how are men to answer to their own consciences, and to that God who is the author of the Bible, for so doing? And after all, what is to be the ultimate rule of the divine proceedings, in regard to us? Are we at our own disposal? Or are we in the hands of an *almighty* God? Are *our* views and conceptions to be the rule of his dealings with us; or are *his own* views of right and wrong, of merit and desert, to guide his disposal of us and ours? Supposing, then, that with the utmost confidence we cherish and advocate principles, in regard to the administration of the divine government, which in the end turn out to be inconsistent with the statutes of heaven as contained in the Bible; what influence will our belief and opinions have on the eternal Judge, in the great day of retribution? Can they have any? And if not, of what avail is it for us to argue and decide, independently of the Bible, and to risk our eternal salvation on conclusions which are made out in this manner?

I would hope that such considerations as these, may have a tendency to check the proneness of some minds, to indulge in *a priori* speculations on this great subject; and may help in persuading them, to lend a listening ear to any serious and impartial attempt, to describe the real state of Scripture testimony in regard to it.

§ 1. *Αἰών* and *Αἰώνιος*.

For the subject of the present investigation,* I have chosen only one word, or (more correctly perhaps) only one species of words, used by the writers of the New Testament. It is in the New Testament that 'life and immortality are brought to light;' and it is there too, that we may of course expect the state and duration of either reward or punishment in the future world, to be most fully and clearly revealed. I seek not doubtful evidence. I aim to exhibit that which is, or ought to be, convincing. At least, I intend to exhibit that which my own mind is unable to resist; and which, I would hope, may assist others in their inquiries relative to our subject.

The words that I have selected for present investigation, are *αἰών* and *αἰώνιος*, commonly translated *forever, ever, eternal, everlasting*; specially so translated, when they are connected with objects that relate to the invisible world. I have been induced to select these words, because I have, at various times, and specially of late, met with not a few speculations and criticisms on them, which are singular, and (in my view) widely departing from the sober rules of legitimate interpretation. I have seen, to my deep regret, many remarks on this awful subject, which seem to betray much levity and inconsideration of mind; and not a few, also, which disclose a resolute determination, (come what will of the laws of exegesis), to support notions on the subject of a future state, that have been adopted independently of Scriptural inquiry, and seem to be maintained in spite of all which the Bible has declared.

I hope I shall not expose myself to censure here, by speaking thus respecting criticisms of this nature. I would not treat with disregard any opinion in theology

---

* This refers only to the *first* Essay in the present Volume.

or criticism, which appears to be the offspring of serious investigation and real effort to seek after the truth, although its author may have greatly mistaken the path of truth. But when I see rash and adventurous criticisms thrown out before the public, which are evidently the offspring neither of patient investigation, nor yet of a serious desire to know what the Bible has decided, but intended only to remove the difficulties which the Scriptures throw in the way of opinions entertained by the authors of such criticisms, and to lull the consciences of men who are uneasy about the subject of future punishment, I feel constrained at least to make an effort, to bring before the public a full investigation of the meaning of the words in question, and to afford them, if it be in my power, more easy and ample means of judging in regard to the criticisms above named, than is afforded by any of the popular works now generally read.

I must advertise my readers, that in order to do this, I cannot confine myself to a merely *popular* exhibition of the evidence with regard to the words in question. Their importance in respect to the great subject of a future state, all must acknowledge who have any good acquaintance with the Scriptures. They form, indeed, the *leading* testimony in regard to the evidence which respects the duration of future punishment. But then, let it be remembered also, they are far from constituting the *only* testimony of the Scriptures, in respect to this subject. I desire that this may be very explicitly understood. It is not my design, for the present, to aim at adducing *all* the evidence relative to future punishment which the Scriptures afford, but only to examine one important part of it; and this, because it has of late been so often drawn into question.

§ 1. *Αἰών* and *Αἰώνιος*.

It will be easily seen by every intelligent reader, that I cannot appeal to the Scriptural usage of the words *αἰών* and *αἰώνιος*, in such a way as to make the investigation a fundamental one, without a reference throughout to the original Scriptures. These are the only legitimate source of *ultimate* appeal, in all controverted subjects of religion. It is to these, indeed, that such of the advocates of universal salvation as are able to do it, profess to make an appeal. I must, therefore, take the same ground; and yet, while I do this, I would hope to make myself intelligible in most cases to all well-educated readers, although they do not possess a knowledge of the *Original*. A few things must, in an investigation like the present, necessarily be without the circle of their apprehension. But I would fain hope, that this will not detract from the general impression which the present essay is designed to make.

In pursuing the inquiry about the Scriptural meaning of *αἰών* and *αἰώνιος* (*for ever* and *everlasting*), I propose to investigate, *the meaning of these words among profane Greek writers; their meaning in the New Testament; the meaning of the corresponding words in the Old Testament, which have been translated by αἰών and αἰώνιος; the meaning of these last words in the Septuagint; then to present a brief view of the bearing, which the testimony exhibited in respect to these words has on the duration of future punishment; and lastly, to make some remarks on the abuse of these words, and on some mistaken criticisms with regard to them.*

§ 2. *Classical use of the words in question.*

Respecting this, there can be but little or no doubt. *Αἰών* means, (1) *Length* or *space of time;* and so, *time of life, age of man, age* considered as a space of time. (2) *Long time, eternity, long indefinite space of time.* These are the usual significations of the word, as given by those excellent lexicographers, Schneider and Passow. There is a third *unusual* meaning sometimes attached to this word, viz. *mark*, which has no bearing on our present inquiry, and seems to have arisen from a mistaken derivation of the word from *ἀΐω, to notice, to mark.*

The word *αἰώνιος*, as defined by Passow, means *long-continuing, everlasting, eternal;* and with this Schneider agrees.

Most of the shades of meaning which these words have in the classics, are also given to them in Scriptural usage; and along with these, some others also which are peculiar to the writers of Hebrew-Greek. No one acquainted with the nature of this Greek, will wonder at this. A great proportion of the Greek words employed in the New Testament and the Septuagint, is used in a similar manner. Not only do they bear many senses foreign to *classic* usage, but many of them are employed in a manner wholly foreign to the Greek classical authors. If any one desires proof of this—overwhelming proof—he has only to inspect a few pages of Schleusner, or of Wahl's Lexicon of the New Testament, which will solve all his doubts.

§ 3. *The meaning of the words in question, as employed by the writers of the New Testament.*

On this inquiry, of course, depends substantially the issue of the question before us. I must beg my readers therefore to have patience, and to bear with me while I endeavor to conduct them, step by step, through every instance in which the words αἰών and αἰώνιος are employed in the New Testament.

There are shorter methods of dispatching the subject in hand; and these are, either to decide it by affirming positively in regard to it, and substituting this for a labored process of proof; or by producing a few instances which may seem to support the theory advanced by any writer, and neglecting the rest; or lastly, by conjecturing what the words in question *ought to mean*, instead of proving what they do mean.

But as I have engaged in the severe task of endeavoring to make a thorough examination, I cannot knowingly adopt either of these methods. I have endeavored to take a view of the *whole* ground for myself; and I am now desirous to submit the results of this labor to the inspection of others, who are willing seriously and laboriously to inquire, what they ought to believe in respect to the momentous subject before us.

If there be any *future* punishment, it belongs of course to a *future state*, i. e. to the invisible world. Our first inquiry then will naturally be, In what sense are the words αἰών and αἰώνιος employed, *when used with reference to the things of the invisible world?*

I omit all those cases in which these words are connected with the subject of *punishment*, for the present. I shall inquire, first of all, how they are employed in regard to all other things belonging to the invisible world, i. e. to all other objects which exist there, or to transactions, occurrencies, condition, or circumstances, belonging to that world.

§ 4. *Meaning of Αἰών.*
FIRST GENERAL CLASS OF MEANINGS.

As the most common and appropriate meaning of *αἰών*, in the New Testament, and the one which best accords with the corresponding Hebrew word עוֹלָם, (which the Septuagint nearly always renders by *αἰών*), and which therefore deserves the first rank in regard to *order*, I put down,

(1) *An indefinite period of time; time without limitation; ever, forever, time without end, eternity;* all in relation to the future.

As to the various instances now to be cited, the reader will see, that some one or other of these shades of meaning applies to all. If he be accustomed to philological and exegetical studies, he will also perceive, that so far as the simple idea of the word *αἰών* is concerned, the sense of it is substantially the same, in *all* the cases now to be designated ; and that the different shades by which the word is rendered, depend on the object with which *αἰών* is associated, or to which it has a relation, rather than on any differences in the real meaning of *αἰών* itself. The idea which this word preserves through the whole, is that of *unlimited, indefinite time;* which, in one case, in consequence of its connection, must be rendered *ever*, (joined with a negative, *never*); in another, *forever*, etc., in all the various ways already mentioned above.

To the following instances I now make the appeal, in confirmation of what has just been stated.

(*a*) I begin with those which have reference to God, (or to Christ), to what belongs to him, or is rendered, or will be rendered to him, and which (from his nature and the

§ 4. Meaning of Αἰών.

nature of things) cannot be supposed ever to have an end, or ever to cease from existing, or from being rendered, etc.

Rom. 1: 25, the Creator, who is blessed *forever*, εἰς τοὺς αἰῶνας· surely, not merely for a period which is to have an end!

Rom. 9: 5, God over all, blessed *forever*, εἰς τοὺς αἰῶνας· plainly in the same sense as above.

Rom. 11: 36, to whom be glory *for ever*, εἰς τοὺς αἰῶνας.

Rom. 16: 27, to the only wise God . . . . be glory *forever*, εἰς τοὺς αἰῶνας.

2 Cor. 11: 31, God . . . who is blessed *forever*, εἰς τοὺς αἰῶνας.

Gal. 1: 5, to whom [God] be glory *forever and ever*, εἰς τοὺς αἰῶνας τῶν αἰώνων.

Eph. 3: 21, to him [God] be glory . . . . to all the generations *of the age of ages* or *of eternity*, τοῦ αἰῶνος τῶν αἰώνων· i. e. to him be eternal glory. The form of expression is plainly *intensive* here.

Phil. 4: 20, to God . . . . be glory *forever and ever*, εἰς τοὺς αἰῶνας τῶν αἰώνων.

1 Tim. 1: 17, to God . . . . be glory *for ever and ever*, εἰς τοὺς αἰῶνας τῶν αἰώνων.

2 Tim. 4: 18, to whom [to the Lord] be glory *forever and ever*, εἰς τοὺς αἰῶνας τῶν αἰώνων.

Heb. 13: 21, to him [God, or Christ] be glory *forever and ever*, εἰς τοὺς αἰῶνας τῶν αἰώνων.

1 Pet. 1: 25, the word of the Lord abideth *forever*, εἰς τὸν αἰῶνα.

1 Pet. 4: 11, to whom [God, or Christ] be glory and praise *forever and ever*, εἰς τοὺς αἰῶνας τῶν αἰώνων.

1 Pet. 5: 11, to him [God] be glory and praise *forever and ever*, εἰς τοὺς αἰῶνας αῶν αἰώνων.

§ 4. Meaning of Αἰών.

2 Pet. 3: 18, to him [Christ] be glory both now and *forever*, νῦν καὶ εἰς ἡμέραν αἰῶνος.

Rev. 1: 6, to him [to God] be glory and praise *forever and ever*, εἰς τοὺς αἰῶνας τῶν αἰώνων.

Rev. 1: 18, and behold! I [Christ] live *forever and ever*, εἰς τοὺς αἰῶνας τῶν αἰώνων.

Rev. 4: 9, glory and honour . . . . to him [God, or Christ], who liveth *forever and ever*, εἰς τοὺς αἰῶνας τῶν αἰώνων.

Rev. 4: 10, they worshipped him [God, or Christ] who liveth *forever and ever*, εἰς τοὺς αἰῶνας τῶν αἰώνων.

Rev. 7: 12, blessing and glory . . . . to our God *for ever and ever*, εἰς τοὺς αἰῶνας τῶν αἰώνων.

Rev. 10: 6, [the angel] sware by him who liveth *forever and ever*, εἰς τοὺς αἰῶνας τῶν αἰώνων.

Rev. 15: 7, vials filled with the wrath of God, who liveth *forever and ever*, εἰς τοὺς αἰῶνας τῶν αἰώνων.

(*b*) The second class of texts under the present general head, are those which have reference to *the happiness of the pious*, especially to their *happiness in heaven* or *the future world*.

Of this tenor are the following; viz.

John 6: 51, if any one eat of this bread, he shall live *forever*, εἰς τὸν αἰῶνα· i. e. he shall be happy always, without end.

John 6: 58, the same expression, in the same sense.

John 8: 51, if any one shall keep my word, he shall *never* see death, οὐ . . . . εἰς τὸν αἰῶνα· by which expression, the *never-ending* happiness of the righteous is surely designated.

§ 4. Meaning of *Αἰών*.

John 8: 52, he shall *never* taste of death, οὐ . . . . εἰς τὸν αἰῶνα· in the same sense as in the preceding example.

John 10: 28, they shall *never* perish, οὐ . . . . εἰς τὸν αἰῶνα· where the endless happiness of the righteous is clearly asserted.

John 11: 26, he that believeth in me shall *never* die, οὐ . . . . εἰς τὸν αἰῶνα· to the same purpose as the above example.

2 Cor. 9: 9, his righteousness abideth *forever*, εἰς τὸν αἰῶνα· i. e. his charitable benevolence shall be eternally rewarded.

1 John 2: 17, he who doeth the will of God, shall abide *forever*, εἰς τὸν αἰῶνα· i. e. he shall ever be secure and happy.

Rev. 22: 5, they [the servants of God] shall reign *forever and ever*, εἰς τοὺς αἰῶνας τῶν αἰώνων· i. e. shall occupy a station of exalted dignity and happiness forever.

(*c*) Another application of *αἰών*, in a sense that classes under our first general head, is, to designate *a period unlimited* or *without bounds*, i. e. *ever*, and (with a negative) *never*. This is clear from the following examples; viz.

Matt. 21: 19, let there be no fruit of thee *forever*, εἰς τὸν αἰῶνα. The words have respect to the fig tree which was cursed. That an *unlimited*, i. e. *endless period* is here meant, seems very plain; for it has respect to all future time.

Mark 11: 14, the same words, in the same sense.

Mark 3: 29, whoever shall blaspheme against the Holy Ghost, shall *never* have forgiveness, οὐκ . . . . εἰς τὸν αἰῶνα. Comp. under No. 4. *a*. Matt. 12: 32.

§ 4. *Meaning of Αἰών.*

Luke 1: 33, he (Jesus) shall reign over the house of David *forever*, εἰς τοὺς αἰῶνας. There may be some difference of opinion here, as to the class of meanings to which the phrase εἰς τοὺς αἰῶνας, is to be assigned. The majority of interpreters give to it the sense of *forever*, and appeal to the nature of the Messiah's kingdom, and also to the corresponding assertion in the latter part of v. 33, " of his kingdom there shall be *no end*, οὐκ .... τέλος." On the other hand, interpreters who construe εἰς τοὺς αἰῶνας somewhat differently, appeal to 1 Cor. 15: 24—28, in order to shew that the kingdom of the Messiah is to have an end, and that therefore the expression in question is to be regarded only as designating *an indefinite period, a very long time.* They add, too, that the passage in Luke plainly has a relation to the kingdom of Christ *as Messiah;* a kingdom which must cease, of course, when the office of Messiah ceases, which will be after the general judgement, 1 Cor. 15: 24—28. The reasoning of the latter seems to be weighty; and I should feel bound to accede to it, unless it might be said, with propriety, that there is a *spiritual* kingdom, one *purely of a moral kind* and adapted to the heavenly world, that will continue after the appropriate reign of Jesus *as Messiah* shall cease. This is certainly favoured by those passages in the New Testament, which ascribe *endless* dominion and power to the Son of God in the same manner as to the Father; e. g. Rev. 5: 13. 11: 15. Heb. 1: 8. On the whole, I am rather inclined to class εἰς τοὺς αἰῶνας here, with those passages which designate an *unlimited period;* particularly because of the οὐκ .... τέλος, which follows in the same verse. Yet I should not be very confident in maintaining this classification, for the reasons stated above.

§ 4. Meaning of Αἰών.

If I am correct, the passage might be classed under (*a*) above.

Luke 1: 55, [God] remembered mercy to Abraham and his seed *forever*, ἕως αἰῶνος; i. e. he *always, ever* has remembered, and *ever* will remember, mercy to Abraham and his seed; he is unchangeably and *perpetually* propitious to them. This text might be referred, also, to the class (*b*) above.

John 4: 14, whoever shall drink of the water which I shall give him, shall *never* thirst, οὐ . . . . εἰς τὸν αἰῶνα; a full negative, and for a period plainly without any limitation. This also might be referred to the class (*b*) above.

John 8: 35, the servant abideth not *forever*, εἰς τὸν αἰῶνα, but the Son abideth *forever*, εἰς τὸν αἰῶνα. Here an unlimited period, a time that has no bounds, is plainly designated.

John 12: 34, we have heard out of the law, that Christ abideth *forever*, εἰς τὸν αἰῶνα. The passage expresses the opinion of the Jews in regard to the Messiah, who, they supposed, would be altogether exempt from death. Of course αἰῶνα here means, *an unlimited* or *endless period*.

John 13: 8, thou shalt *never* wash my feet, οὐ . . . εἰς τὸν αἰῶνα.

John 14: 16, that he [the Comforter] may abide with you *forever*, εἰς τὸν αἰῶνα. Here *always*, i. e. constantly and for an unlimited time, is plainly the idea conveyed by εἰς τὸν αἰῶνα.

1 Cor. 8: 13, I will *never* eat flesh, οὐ . . . . εἰς τὸν αἰῶνα.

Heb. 1: 8, thy throne, O God, is *forever and ever*, εἰς τὸν αἰῶνα τοῦ αἰῶνος. The idea which this expresses, seems to be the same as that in Luke 1: 33 above; which

§ 4. *Meaning of Αἰών.*

see. It may be remarked here, in confirmation of what will be said by and by about the use of the singular and plural number, that εἰς τὸν αἰῶνα τοῦ αἰῶνος differs not at all, in *sense*, from εἰς τους αἰῶνας τῶν αἰώνων.

Heb. 5: 6, thou art a high priest *forever*, εἰς τὸν αἰῶνα· i. e. for a period unlimited, undefined, a very long period; *forever*, while the nature of things shall permit or require this office.

Heb. 6: 20, Jesus . . . . made high priest *for ever*, εἰς τὸν αἰῶνα· in the same sense as above.

Heb. 7: 17, thou art a priest *forever*, εἰς τὸν αἰῶνα· in the same sense as before.

Heb. 7: 21, the same expression, in the same sense.

Heb. 7: 24, but he, because he remaineth [a priest] *forever*, εἰς τὸν αἰῶνα· in reference to the same subject as the three last examples above.

Heb. 7: 28, but the word of the oath . . . maketh the Son [high priest], who is exalted to a state of glory *forever*, εἰς τὸν αἰῶνα. This might be ranked under No. 1. *b;* but I have chosen to arrange it here, in consequence of its intimate connection with the four preceding texts.

Heb. 13: 8, Jesus Christ the same yesterday, to day, and *forever*, εἰς τοὺς αἰῶνας· i. e. Jesus Christ invariably, always the same.

2 John v. 2, [the truth] shall be with you *always*, εἰς τὸν αἰῶνα.

Rev. 5: 12, to Him that sitteth on the throne, and to the LAMB, be . . . . glory and power *forever and ever*, εἰς τοὺς αἰῶνας τῶν αἰώνων. This might be ranged under (*a*) above.

Rev. 11: 15, he [Christ] shall reign *forever and ever*, εἰς τοὺς αἰῶνας τῶν αἰώνων. See on Luke 1: 33 above.

§ 4. Meaning of Αἰών.

Thus far all the examples which have been cited, refer to FUTURE TIME. But there is another small class of examples, in which αἰών refers to PAST TIME, and which require a distinct head of enumeration. They are of a nature kindred with the various species of meaning already mentioned under No. 1. *a. b. c;* and therefore I shall designate them here as belonging to No. 2, under the general arrangement. I observe then,

(2) That αἰών sometimes means, *an indefinite* or *long period in time past, ancient days, times of old, long ago, always in time past, generations* or *ages long since.*

Of this tenor are the following passages; viz.

Luke 1: 70, as he [God] promised by the mouth of his holy prophets *in ancient times,* or of his holy prophets *long ago,* ἀπ᾽ αἰῶνος.

Acts 15: 18, Known unto God *of old,* απ᾽ αἰῶνος, are all his works; i. e. God knew all his works from the most ancient times, or always in times past.

1 Cor. 2: 7, which God decreed *long ago* or *ages since,* πρὸ τῶν αἰώνων· i. e. from eternity.

Eph. 3: 9, the mystery hidden in God *from ages,* ἀπὸ τῶν αἰώνων· i. e. hidden during all ages past, or always hidden during ages past.

Eph. 3: 11, according to the purpose *of ages,* τῶν αἰώνων· i. e. according to the ancient or eternal purpose.

Col. 1: 26, the mystery hidden *from ages,* ἀπὸ τῶν αἰώνων· in the same sense as Eph. 3: 9 above.

Under this head also should be classed John 9: 32, *never* was it heard, ἐκ τοῦ αἰῶνος οὐκ ἠκούσθη, that one opened the eyes of him that was born blind; i. e. during all ages past, or from the most ancient time, such a thing has not been heard of.

§ 4. *Meaning of Aἰών.*

The cases which I shall next rank under No. 3, may not appear, at first view, to be very nearly related to those already exhibited. But the experienced interpreter will easily perceive, that there is in them a tacit reference to the idea of *age, period of time, seculum ;* and also, that this has particular reference to quantity of time as a whole, and may relate either to a *past*, or a *future* age. In accordance with this, then, we may say,

(3) That *αἰών* occasionally means, *age* in the sense of *dispensation*, viz. age (Jewish), age (Christian).

In this case, it is obviously employed as we employ the word *age* in English, when we speak of *the patriarchal age, the antediluvian age*, etc. Of this meaning may be found the following examples ; viz.

1 Cor. 10: 11, on whom the ends *of the age* (ages) have come, τῶν αἰώνων· i. e. who live at the close of the Jewish age or dispensation.

Eph. 2: 7, that he might shew *in the ages to come*, ἐν τοῖς αἰῶσι τοῖς ἐπερχομένοις, the exceeding riches of his grace. This may be construed of *the* [gospel] *ages ;* or it may be taken in the general sense of *secula*. The former is consonant with New Testament usage ; but the latter is, perhaps, the more probable sense.

Heb. 6: 5, who have tasted the good promise of God, and the powers *of the age to come*, μέλλοντος αἰῶνος· i. e. of the miraculous powers bestowed under the *gospel dispensation*.

These are all the examples which occur, that require to be ranked under this head ; and of these, Eph. 2. 7 might be ranked under another category, and considered merely as an example of the *classical* sense of *αἰών*, viz. *seculum, aevum, age* simply considered.

§ 5. *Meaning of Αἰών.*

It will be perceived, that most of the meanings of αἰών under the preceding heads, are in accordance with those which the word not unfrequently has in the Greek classic writers. In this respect, however, the New Testament usage differs from the classical one, viz. in that αἰών, in the New Testament, *most usually* means, *an indefinite, unlimited period of time;* whereas in the classics, the sense of *aevum, seculum, age, generation* (in respect to *time*), appears to be its more usual meaning.

§ 5. *Meaning of Αἰών.*

SECOND GENERAL CLASS OF MEANINGS.

I come now to a *secondary* and *peculiar* use of the word in question; one altogether different from any thing in the Greek classics, and derived, as it would seem, entirely from the Hebrew usage of the word עוֹלָם, which the Seventy have translated so uniformly by αἰών.

In the ancient Hebrew Scriptures, the word עוֹלָם properly means, *eternity;* as I shall have occasion by and by to shew. Like αἰών also, it is frequently applied to designate *an indefinite period of time*, which is spoken of in reference to a great variety of objects, and with shades of difference, like those which have been named in regard to the use of αἰών. But the sense of *world, the present world* and *the future world,* (when connected with הַזֶּה *this* and הַבָּא *that which is to come*), is one which does not appear ever to have been attached to עוֹלָם, by the most ancient Hebrew writers; nor is it found in the Hebrew Scriptures, unless it be in Ecc. 3: 11, which is so doubtful, and so much disputed, that no philological conclusions can be safely deduced from it.

In the later Hebrew, however, (i. e. the Talmudic

§ 5. *Meaning of Αἰών.*

and Rabbinic), the word עוֹלָם is employed, in innumerable instances, in the sense of *world;* and this, either as *present world*, or *future world*. From this usage in the *later* Hebrew, (yet not so late but that it preceded the time when the New Testament was written), it comes, that αἰών, in the New Testament, is not unfrequently employed in a similar manner.

No one, who is at all acquainted with the multitude of Hebrew meanings attached to Greek words, both in the Septuagint and in the New Testament, will feel any surprise at this, or hesitate a moment about admitting the possibility or the reality of it. Hence we may assign to αἰών, another meaning different from any above given, viz.

(4) The meaning, *world;* also *present world*, and *future world*, when such qualifying words are joined with it, as shew that it refers to the one or the other.

(*a*) It is sometimes employed to denote the *present world* and *future world*, with special reference to *time* or *duration*, i. e. the period of their existence, or of one's existence in them. Of this character is the word in question in the following passages ; viz.

Matt. 12: 32, [the man who has uttered blasphemy against the Holy Ghost], shall not be forgiven, neither *in this world*, nor in that *which is to come*, οὔτε ἐν τούτῳ τῷ αἰῶνι, οὔτε ἐν τῷ μέλλοντι [αἰῶνι] ; i. e. he shall not be forgiven during his continuance in the present world, nor in that which is to come ; an affirmation plainly added by way of intensity, in order to strengthen the declaration, οὐκ ἀφεθήσεται αὐτῷ, *forgiveness shall not be extended to him*, which immediately precedes.

§ 5. *Meaning of Αἰών.*

Mark 10: 30, [the man who has forsaken all that he might follow Christ], shall receive a hundred fold *in the present time*, ἐν τῷ καιρῷ τούτῳ, and eternal life *in the world to come*, ἐν τῷ αἰῶνι τῷ ἐρχομένῳ. Here αἰών is used for *world*, with special reference to *the period of its duration;* as is plain from its being placed in antithesis with καιρῷ τούτῳ. This might be translated *age* and ranked under No. 3, but with a classical sense like that of Eph. 2: 7.

Luke 18: 30, the same words, in the same sense.

On the whole, all the instances here under *a.*, might be rendered in the same classical way, and make a sense well fitted for the passages in which they stand. If any one prefers this method, I shall not object against it. Thus construed, all these texts, with that of Eph. 2: 7, must be considered as examples of the more common *classical* sense of αἰών.

(*b*) *Αἰών* is sometimes employed to denote *the world with all its cares*, or *business*, or *temptations*, or *allurements to sin*. Just so we often employ it in the English language. *A man of the world*, is a man devoted to the cares or pleasures of the world. In a like sense, the later Hebrew עוֹלָם was often employed.

The examples of such a sense are as follows; viz.

Matt. 13: 22, the cares *of this world*, τοῦ αἰῶνος τούτου . . . . choke the word; i. e. worldly business, occupation, engagements, stifle the impressions which religious truth had made.

Mark 4: 19, the same expression, in the same sense.

Luke 16: 8, the children *of this world*, τοῦ αἰῶνος τούτου, are wiser in their generation, etc.

§ 5. *Meaning of Αἰών.*

Luke 20: 34, the children *of this world*, τοῦ αἰῶνος τούτου, marry, etc.; i. e. worldly men, men devoted to worldly pursuits, etc.

Rom. 12: 2, be not conformed *to this world*, τῷ αἰῶνι τούτῳ· i. e. to the sinful pursuits and pleasures of this world.

1 Cor. 1: 20, where is the disputer *of this world*, τοῦ αἰῶνος τούτο· i. e. the worldly disputer, one who disputes after the manner of men of the world.

1 Cor. 2: 6, but not the wisdom *of this world*, τοῦ αἰῶνος τούτου, i. e. not the wisdom of worldly men; nor of the princes *of this world*, τοῦ αἰῶνος τούτου, i. e. of worldly-minded princes.

1 Cor. 2: 8, which none of the princes *of this world* knew, τοῦ αἰῶνος τούτου· i. e. which no worldly-minded princes knew.

2 Cor. 4: 4, whom the god *of this world*, τοῦ αἰῶνος τούτου, hath blinded; i. e. whom Satan, who reigns in worldly men, hath blinded.

Gal. 1: 4, that he might select us from *the present evil world*, ἐκ τοῦ ἐνεστῶτος αἰῶνος πονηροῦ.

2 Tim. 4: 10, Demas hath forsaken us, having loved *the present world*, τὸν τῦν αἰῶνα.

Tit. 2: 12, let us live soberly and righteously and godly, *in the present world*, ἐν τῷ νῦν αἰῶνι· where the antithesis shews, that *the world of temptation and trial is meant.*

(*c*) From the preceding use of αἰών it comes, that the word is sometimes employed simply to denote *the world itself* as an object or as an actual existence, i. e. simply *mundus*, κόσμος, and this, either *present* or *fu-*

§ 5. Meaning of Αἰών.

ture. Of this, the following seem to be evident examples; viz.

Matt. 13: 40, so shall it be in the end of this world, ἐν τῇ συντελείᾳ τοῦ αἰῶνος τούτου· i. e. when the final consummation of all things shall take place, and the world comes to an end or is destroyed.

Matt. 13: 49, the same words, in the same sense.

Matt. 24: 3, what shall be the sign of thy coming, and *of the end of the world?* τῆς συντελείας τοῦ αἰῶνος, which (as the phrase was used here by the disciples) seems probably to mean, *end of the world* in a sense like that of the two preceding instances.

Matt. 28: 20, I am with you always, *unto the end of the world;* a clear case of the same meaning with the preceding words, as πάσας τὰς ἡμέρας, *always,* plainly shews.

In Matthew, it appears that the usage of αἰών almost throughout, (in passages where the reading is not doubtful), is in accordance with the *later* usage of the Hebrew in respect to the word עוֹלָם. What influence this may have on the critical questions, Whether Matthew wrote his Gospel in Hebrew? and of course, Whether the present Greek is only a translation? I cannot stop here to inquire; but critical readers will not fail to note the circumstance, to which I have now adverted.

Luke 20: 35, they who are counted worthy to obtain *that world,* τοῦ αἰῶνος ἐκείνου· viz. the *future world,* in distinction from αἰῶνος τ ο ύ τ ο υ in the preceding verse, or in opposition to it.

1 Cor. 3: 18, if any man thinketh to be wise among you *in this world,* ἐν τῷ αἰῶνι τούτῳ. In the next verse, κόσμος is put for αἰών. This example might perhaps be referred to No. 4. *b ;* and be taken in this sense, viz. if any worldly-minded man among you, etc.

§ 5. *Meaning of Αἰών*. 31

Eph. 1: 21, above every name .... *in this world, and in that which is to come,* ἐν τῷ αἰῶνι τούτῳ, ἀλλὰ καὶ ἐν τῷ [αἰῶνι] μέλλοντι. This, some may suppose, might be put under No. 4. *a;* but it does not appear that a special relation to *time* is here designated.

1 Tim. 1: 17, now to the king *of the world* (worlds), τῶν αἰώνων· i. e. the king of the earth, or the king of the universe. So in the Old Testament, Ps. 47: 7, *God is king of all the earth.* Zech. 14: 9, *the Lord shall be king over all the earth;* and so, in innumerable places, God is styled *king*, *king of Israel*, etc. That the plural number (αἰώνων) is here employed, makes no difference in the signification; as appears from Heb. 1: 2. 11: 3. The same usage is extended to many other words; e. g. מִשְׁכָּן *tabernacle* and מִשְׁכָּנִים *tabernacles*, אֵל *God* and אֱלֹהִים *God*, יָם *sea* and יַמִּים *seas*, οὐρανός *heaven* and οὐρανοί *heavens*, σάββατον *sabbath* and σάββατα *sabbaths*, etc.; which, (although I have translated some of them in the singular and some in the plural), are *indiscriminately* employed in both numbers, by the sacred writers. *Αἰώνων* then may mean here, as in Heb. 1: 2. 11: 3, *world;* or in all these cases it may be rendered *worlds*, if any one should prefer this. But I am not aware that the Hebrews applied the words עוֹלָם and αἰών, to designate any of the planets except the earth. If so, then the *plural* number here is to be rendered in conformity with the usage above intimated; just as אֶרֶץ *terra* and אֲרָצוֹת *terrae*, עוֹלָם *mundus* and עוֹלָמוֹת *mundi*, are promiscuously used, not unfrequently in one and the same sense.

The objection to construing αἰώνων here as meaning *ages*, is, that the idea of *eternity* or *immortality*, (which would thus be designated by it), is expressed by the very next word which follows, viz. ἀφθάρτῳ, *incorruptible, imperishable, immortal.*

1 Tim. 6: 17, charge them that are rich *in the present world,* ἐν τῷ νῦν αἰῶνι. Without any violence, this might be referred also to the class *b*, which precedes the present head.

Heb. 1: 2, by whom also he made *the world* (worlds), τοὺς αἰῶνας. See on 1 Tim. 1: 17 above, in regard to the use of the plural here.

Heb. 11: 3, by faith we perceive, that *the world* (worlds, τοὺς αἰῶνας), was created by the word of God. See as above.

Nearly all of the above instances are very clear and striking examples of the purely *Hebraistic* sense of the word αἰών, as sometimes employed by the writers of the New Testament.

To the meanings above specified, I now subjoin one which is peculiar, and one, I may add, which is of so doubtful a nature, that no philological conclusions can be safely deduced from it.

§ 6. *Peculiar meaning of Αἰών.*

(5) As דּוֹר, in Hebrew, means *generation of men*, considered either as to the *time* in which they live, or as to the *persons themselves,* so αἰών, in one case, seems, like this word, to have the meaning of *generation,* i. e. *race, progeny, a class of men in existence.*

Of this peculiar meaning, the following appears to be an example ; viz.

Eph. 2: 2, in which [trespasses] ye walked, in accordance *with the generation of this world,* κατὰ τὸν αἰῶνα τοῦ κόσμου τούτου· i. e. according to the course pursued

§ 6. *Meaning of Αἰών.*

by men of this world. The idea is heightened by the writer's adding immediately, "According to the prince of the dominion of the air;" i. e. in accordance with the designs of Satan, who, being supposed by the Jews to dwell in the air, was called *the prince of the air.*

One is almost tempted, here, to adopt the translation *Aeon*, an evil spirit presiding over the wicked world, and called, in the next clause, *the prince of the dominion of the air.* But the uncertainty whether the Gnostic philosophy had yet introduced its speculations about *Aeons* (Αἰῶνες); and particularly, whether this term, in such a sense, was known to any of the writers of the New Testament; seems to forbid such a rendering of αἰῶνα here. I cannot help thinking, that it is safer to build on the analogy which the Hebrew דוֹר affords, and which makes a sense apposite to the subject.

§ 7. *Instances of Αἰών in respect to future punishment.*

(6) Under a distinct head, also, I will now arrange, (for the sake of completing my view of αἰών), the cases which have reference to the punishment of the wicked.

I do not expect the reader to pronounce judgement on this part of the subject here. I have made the present arrangement only for convenience' sake; not designing either to anticipate a judgement in regard to the meaning of αἰών in this connection, or to forestall the opinion of the reader. His judgement may be suspended, for the present, on this class of texts; and he may regard them here simply as a record of facts, i. e. of expressions actually occurring in the New Testament.

2 Pet. 2: 17, to whom [to transgressors] is reserved the blackness of darkness *forever*, εἰς αἰῶνα.

§ 7. *Meaning of Αἰών.*

Jude v. 13, for whom [for the wicked] the blackness of darkness is reserved *forever, εἰς τὸν αἰῶνα.*

Rev. 14: 11, the smoke of their torment, [the torment of those who worship the beast], shall ascend up *forever and ever, εἰς αἰῶνας αἰώνων.*

Rev. 19: 3, and the smoke of her, [of Babylon the mother of abominations], ascendeth up *forever and ever, εἰς τοὺς αἰῶνας τῶν αἰώνων.*

Rev. 20: 10, and they, [the devil, the beast, and the false prophet], shall be tormented continually, *forever and ever, εἰς τοὺς αἰῶνας τῶν αἰώνων.*

These are all the instances of *αἰών* which are found in the New Testament, where the genuineness of the text is unquestionable. All the cases of a questionable nature I have purposely omitted. They cannot be built upon with safety; and dispute about the genuineness of any particular texts, would be quite foreign to my present design. I therefore omit the instances of *αἰών*, in Matt. 6: 13. Rev. 5: 14, which are decidedly rejected by Dr. Knapp as *spurious;* and also the instances in Acts 3: 21. Eph. 1: 12. 1 Pet. 1: 23, which are considered and marked by him as *dubious.*

---

§ 8. *General summary of the meaning of Αἰών.*

The result of the preceding investigation, (excepting the cases of doubtful readings), is as follows; viz.

The whole number of instances in which the word *αἰών* is employed, amounts to 95.

Of these, 16 are used in the ascriptions of praise, glory, honour, blessing, etc. to God and Christ; and in re-

§ 8. *Summary of the meanings of Αἰών.* 35

gard to these, there can be no rational doubt that $αἰών$ designates *a period unlimited* or *never-ending*.

Equally certain is the same meaning, in the 5 cases in which it is applied to God, or to Christ, *who liveth forever.*

In 4 cases, it is employed in designating the dominion of Christ; viz. Luke 1: 33. Heb. 1: 8. Rev. 5: 13, and Rev. 11: 15. But the meaning here may be called in question. See on Luke 1: 33 above, p. 21. As to Rev. 5: 13, I have rendered the word $κράτος$, *power*, Hebrew עֹז ; but as עֹז appears in a few cases to mean *praise, honour*, some may insist on that sense being given to $κράτος$ here. If they should do so, this will not alter the meaning of the $αἰών$ which follows, because it stands connected with *the glory given to God*, as well as to Christ, and therefore, it plainly means *a time unlimited*. The text in Rev. 11: 15, seems to ascribe dominion to Christ in the same sense as Luke 1: 33. Heb. 1: 8; and it may therefore be questioned by some, whether *eternal* dominion be here meant.

In *one* case, 1 Pet. 1: 25, it is said of the *word of God*, that it abideth *forever ;* which plainly means, that it will *always* be accomplished, or *always* remain stable, certain.

In 9 cases, it is applied to the future happiness of the saints.

In 18 cases, it designates the sense of *ever*, (with a negative) *never, always, without end*, etc.; and in a great majority of these cases, it is applied to something which Christ is, or does.

In 7 cases, it is applied to designate *an indefinite period in ages past, ages long ago, very ancient times.*

In 3 cases, it is applied to designate *age* in the sense of *dispensation*, either Christian or Jewish. But one of these is susceptible of another interpretation.

In 3 cases, it seems to designate *the world present* or

§ 8. *Summary of the meanings of Αἰών.*

future, considered with special reference to a period of duration, i. e. with the adsignification of *continuance*.

In 12 cases, it designates *the world*, as the scene or place of cares, trials, enticements to sin, etc.

In 11 cases, it seems to designate, more simply, *the world* present or future, considered merely as a place of residence for men, as an object of real existence, etc.

In one case, Eph. 2: 2, it seems to be equivalent to the Hebrew word דּוֹר, and to designate the idea of *generation, homines saeculi hujus, genus hominum.*

In 5 cases, it is applied to the subject of future punishment.

In comparing these cases together, it appears that those which have a simple respect to time, i. e. to *time future*, are employed in the sense of *unlimited time, indefinite time, ever, always, forever,* etc. Of this number are 49, besides the *five* cases which relate to future punishment, and the *four* which relate to the Messiah's kingdom.

Only *seven* cases of αἰών have relation to *time past;* and these designate either *a period from eternity*, or *ages long ago, very ancient times.*

The *four* cases which relate to the dominion of Christ, may be understood variously, by different interpreters who disagree about his nature or his dominion. The passages are noted above. At least, these cases must designate a future *indefinite period.*

All the other cases of αἰών (of which there are 30), may be classed under the general signification of the Hebrew word עוֹלָם, (as employed in the Talmudic and Rabbinic Hebrew), viz. *world* in some sense or other, either present or future, Jewish or Christian. Of these, there are *four* shades of meaning, viz. *world*, in reference to

§ 8. *Summary of the meanings of Αἰων.*

the period of time which it comprises, of which there are 3 cases; or *world*, in reference to its cares, pleasures, enticements, etc., of which there are 12 cases; or *world* as a place of abode, an existing, real object etc., of which there are 11 cases; or, finally *world* Jewish or Christian, i. e. dispensation, of which there are 3 cases. I leave Eph. 2: 2, out of the account here, as the instance is so peculiar.

We come then, by virtue of this examination, to the conclusion, that whenever αἰών is employed for the purpose merely of designating *future time*, as a *period of duration*, it designates an *indefinite unlimited time* in all cases; (those of future punishment being for the present excepted). In nearly all, it designates *a period in the most absolute and extensive sense unlimited;* as in the 49 cases mentioned above, independently of those which have relation to future punishment, and those which relate to the Messiah's kingdom.

The use of αἰών in order to designate *past time*, is seldom in the New Testament, as the above examples shew; there being only *seven* cases in the whole. Of these, *six* relate clearly to an *indefinite, unlimited period in ages past*, i. e. they signify *eternity a parte ante*, as the elder theological writers were wont to call it. Of this tenor most clearly are Acts 15: 18. 1 Cor. 2: 7. Eph. 3: 9. 3: 11. Col. 1: 26. See above, under signification No. 2. In one case only, αἰών means *long ago, in ancient times* simply, viz. in Luke 1: 80; in one case, with the negative οὐκ, John 9: 32, it means *never*.

We have, then, at least 55 instances in the New Testament, in which αἰών certainly means, *an unlimited period of duration* either future or past, *ever, always;* omit-

§ 8. *Summary of the meanings of Αἰών.*

ting the cases in which it respects future punishment, and those which have regard to the dominion of the Messiah. If these be included, we have 64 cases, (out of the whole 94 which occur), in which αἰών means *unlimited period, boundless duration.*

Unless we except Luke 1: 70, (which however can hardly be excepted, it being a clear case of employing αἰών in a manner designating an *indefinite* kind of period), there is no case in which αἰών is employed in order to designate simply a *definite, limited period,* in all the New Testament ; I mean, there is no case of this nature, where αἰών is employed with the intention of conveying the simple idea of *duration,* or *time during which any thing shall continue to exist* or *to be done.* The New Testament writers employ ἡλικία and γενεά, to designate simply the age or period of men's lives. In no case is αἰών employed by them simply in this sense ; or at most, we can except only Eph. 2: 7.

It is clear then, that whenever αἰών simply marks time in the New Testament, it marks *indefinite, unlimited time,* and such only. In some very few cases, there are circumstances accompanying the use of it, which shew that eternity, in the absolute and simple sense of the word, cannot be intended. But an overwhelming majority of cases designate *eternity a parte post,* (as the technical expression is), i. e. *a future period without any limits* or *bounds.*

In regard to the other sense of αἰών, (i. e. its meaning when it is not primarily designed to mark *time*), it is plainly derived, as has been shewn above (p. 420 seq.), from the later Hebrew עוֹלָם , in the sense of *world;* and it is employed merely to designate this, with the adsignifications of *continuance,* or of *cares, business, pleasures,*

§ 9. *Meaning of Αἰώνιος.* 39

etc.; or else to designate *world* simply as a place of residence, action, etc.; or world Christian or Jewish. All these meanings are obviously foreign to the question about future punishment; with the exception of those, however, which speak of the *future world, the world to come*, as the abode of sinners in their state of retribution. Of these, more hereafter.

We are now prepared to advance to the investigation of the second word in question, viz. αἰώνιος.

ΑΙΩΝΙΟΣ.

This is plainly a derivate of αἰών, according to the common laws of the Greek language. The question of course will now come up, Whether αἰώνιος the *adjective*, corresponds in meaning throughout with αἰών the *substantive?*

The classical sense of this word, as given by Passow, is *long-continued, everlasting, eternal;* all, of course, designating *an indefinite* or *unlimited period*, and agreeing with the meaning of αἰών, in all those cases which have a simple relation to time.

The *ancient* Hebrew has no corresponding adjective here; but it employs the noun עוֹלָם in the place of one, as is usual in a multitude of cases with this ancient language. But the later Talmudic and Rabbinic Hebrew employs an adjective formed from עוֹלָם, (just as the Greek αἰώνιος is derived from αἰών), in the sense of *perpetuus, eternus, sempiternus, perpetual, eternal, everlasting*. The adjective is עוֹלָמִי. It is somewhat remarkable, also, that although only the later Hebrew employs the word עוֹלָם in the sense of *world*, as above described,

40 § 9. *Meaning of Αἰώνιος.*

yet this same Hebrew, which alone employs the adjective עוֹלָמִי, never uses it in the sense of *worldly* etc., but only in the sense of *eternal, everlasting.*

We shall see that in this respect, also, the Greek adjective αἰώνιος corresponds, in the New Testament, almost uniformly with the Hebrew adjective עוֹלָמִי ; and that all the uses of αἰώνιος correspond with the *first* class of significations which αἰών bears, and not with the Hebrew-Greek meaning of it.

We come now to the usage of the word, as exhibited in the New Testament.

§ 10. *Meaning of Αἰώνιος.*

First general class of meanings.

(1) It signifies *perpetual, never-ending, eternal.*

(*a*) It is so employed, *in regard to the happiness of the righteous.*

Matt. 19: 16, what good thing shall I do, that I may inherit *eternal life*, ζωὴν αἰώνιον.

Matt. 19: 29, whoever shall forsake houses, or brethren . . . . for my sake, shall receive . . . . *eternal life*, ζωὴν αἰώνιον.

Matt. 25: 46, but the righteous [shall go away] into *everlasting life*, ζωὴν αἰώνιον.

Mark 10: 17, the same as Matt. 19: 16 above.

Mark 10: 30, the same as Matt. 19: 29 above.

Luke 10: 25, like the case in Matt. 19: 16 above.

Luke 16: 9, that when ye fail [die], ye may be received into *eternal mansions*, εἰς τὰς αἰωνίους σκηνάς· i. e. into eternal abodes of happiness, comp. John 14: 2.

Luke 18: 18, the same as Matt. 19: 16 above.

§ 10. Meaning of Αἰώνιος.

Luke 18: 30, the same as Matt. 19: 29 above.

John 3: 15, he that believeth on him [Christ], ... shall have *eternal life*, ζωὴν αἰώνιον.

John 3: 16, that whosoever believeth on him [Christ], . . . should have *eternal life*, ζωὴν αἰώνιον.

John 3: 36, he who believeth on the Son, hath *eternal life*, ζωὴν αἰώνιον.

John 4: 14, it shall be in him a well of water, springing up *to eternal life*, εἰς ζωὴν αἰώνιον.

John 4: 36, he shall gather fruit *to eternal life*, εἰς ζωὴν αἰώνιον.

John 5: 24, he who believeth on him that sent me, hath *eternal life*, ζωὴν αἰώνιον.

John 5; 39, by them ye think ye have *eternal life*, ζωὴν αἰώνιον.

John 6: 27, labour for the meat which endureth *to eternal life*, εἰς ζωὴν αἰώνιον.

John 6: 40, he who believeth on him [Christ], shall have *eternal life*, ζωὴν αἰώνιον.

John 6: 47, he who believeth on me [Christ], hath *eternal life*, ζωὴν αἰώνιον.

John 6: 54, he who drinketh my blood hath *eternal life*, ζωὴν αἰώνιον.

John 6: 68, thou hast the words *of eternal life*, ζωῆς αἰωνίου.

John 10: 28, I give *eternal life* to them, ζωὴν αἰώνιον.

John 12: 25, he who hateth his present life, shall preserve it [his soul] *for eternal life*, εἰς ζωὴν αἰώνιον.

John 12: 50, I know that his commandment is *eternal life*, ζωὴ αἰώνιος· i. e. the keeping of his commandment leads to eternal happiness.

John 17: 2, that he [Jesus] might give to them [his disciples] *eternal life*, ζωὴν αἰώνιον.

§ 10. Meaning of Αἰώνιος.

John 17: 3, this is *eternal life*, ζωὴ αἰώνιος.

Acts 13: 46, ye have judged yourselves to be unworthy *of eternal life*, ζωῆς αἰωνίου.

Acts 13: 48, and as many believed as were ordained *to eternal life*, εἰς ζωὴν αἰώνιον.

Rom. 2: 7, to them . . . . who seek for glory . . . . [God will give] *eternal life*, ζωὴν αἰώνιον.

Rom. 5: 21, so shall grace reign . . . . *unto eternal life*, εἰς ζωὴν αἰώνιον.

Rom. 6: 22, ye have the end [of obedience], *eternal life*, ζωὴν αἰώνιον.

Rom. 6: 23, the gift of God is *eternal life*, ζωὴ αἰώνιος.

2 Cor. 4: 17, a far more exceeding and *eternal weight* of glory, αἰώνιον βάρος δόξης.

Gal. 6: 8, he who soweth to the spirit, shall of the spirit reap *life everlasting*, ζωὴν αἰώνιον.

2 Thess. 2: 16, God . . . . who hath loved us and given us *eternal consolation*, αἰώνιον παράκλησιν.

1 Tim. 1: 16, an example for those who should believe in him *unto eternal life*, εἰς ζωὴν αἰώνιον.

1 Tim. 6: 12, lay hold on *eternal life*, τῆς αἰωνίου ζωῆς.

2 Tim. 2: 10, *with eternal glory*, μετὰ δόξης αἰωνίου.

Tit. 1: 1, in hope of *eternal life*, ζωῆς αἰωνίου.

Tit. 3: 7, that we might be heirs, according to the hope *of eternal life*, ζωῆς αἰωνίου.

Heb. 5: 9, he became the author of *eternal salvation*, σωτηρίας αἰωνίου.

Heb. 9: 12, he obtained *eternal redemption* for us, αἰώνιον λύτρωσιν.

Heb. 9: 15, that they who are chosen might receive *the eternal inheritance*, τῆς αἰωνίου κληρονομίας.

1 Pet. 5: 10, God . . . . who called us *unto his eternal glory*, εἰς τὴν αἰώνιον αὐτοῦ δόξαν.

§ 10. *Meaning of Αἰώνιος.*

2 Pet. 1: 11, an entrance into *the eternal kingdom,* εἰς τὴν αἰώνιον βασιλείαν.

1 John 2: 25, he hath promised to us *eternal life,* ζωὴν αἰώνιον.

1 John 3: 15, no murderer hath *eternal life,* ζωὴν αἰώνιον.

1 John 5: 11, God hath given to us *eternal life,* ζωὴν αἰώνιον.

1 John 5: 13, those who believe have *eternal life,* ζωὴν αἰώνιον.

1 John 5: 20, the same is the true God and *eternal life,* ἡ ζωὴ αἰώνιος.

Jude v. 21, expecting the mercy of our Lord Jesus Christ, *unto eternal life,* εἰς ζωὴν αἰώνιον.

(*b*) The next class of cases are those *which have respect to God or his glory.*

Rom. 16: 26, according to the commandment *of the eternal God,* τοῦ αἰωνίου θεοῦ.

1 Tim. 6: 16, to whom [to God] be honour and *everlasting praise,* κράτος αἰώνιον. Here κράτος=עֹז.

(*c*) There are a few solitary, and *miscellaneous* cases, which I shall arrange under one head.

2 Cor. 4: 18, the things which are not seen, are *eternal,* αἰώνια.

2 Cor. 5: 1, we have a habitation not made with hands, *eternal,* αἰώνιον, in the heavens. This might be arranged under (*a*) above.

In Heb. 9: 14, it is applied to the Spirit, (either of Christ or of God); who by *an eternal Spirit* offered up himself, etc., διὰ πνεύματος αἰωνίου.

44   §§ 10, 11. *Meaning of Αἰώνιος.*

Heb. 13: 20, the blood of an *everlasting covenant*, διαθήκης αἰωνίου· i. e. of a covenant *never* to be changed or abrogated.

1 John 1: 2, we declare unto you *the eternal life*, ζωὴν αἰώνιον· viz. Jesus the author of eternal life.

Rev. 14: 6, an angel . . . . having *the everlasting gospel*, εὐαγγέλιον αἰώνιον.

In Philemon v. 15, αἰώνιον is used adverbially, in the sense of *forever, always.*

§ 11. SECOND GENERAL CLASS OF MEANINGS.

(2) In *three* cases, the word αἰώνιος seems to bear a sense kindred to that of αἰών under No. 2 above, viz. *ancient, long since, very early, remote.*

The following are the examples of this sort, viz.

Rom. 16: 25, the revelation of the mystery, which was kept in silence *in ancient ages*, χρόνοις αἰωνίοις· i. e. during all preceding ages, or always hitherto, from eternity.

2 Tim. 1: 9, according to his own purpose, and the grace given us through Jesus Christ, *before the ancient ages*, πρὸ χρόνων αἰωνίων· i. e. before the primitive ages, which means, before the world began, from eternity. Thus in John 17: 5, the glory which I had with thee, *before the world was*, obviously means, *from eternity.* So our English version, in 2 Tim. 1: 9, *before the world began*, πρὸ χρόνων αἰωνίων, which is also repeated in Tit. 1: 2, where the Greek expression is the same as here.

Tit. 1: 2, eternal life, which God, who cannot lie, promised *before the ancient ages*, πρὸ χρόνων αἰωνίων· evidently in the same sense as the phrase above.

§ 12. *Meaning of Αἰώνιος*.

These are all the instances in the New Testament, which have relation to *past* time; and these, it is very evident, have an intimate connection with the use of αἰών in No. 2 above.

There remain,

§ 12. *Instances in respect to future punishment*.

(3) The instances where αἰώνιος is used with relation to future punishment, are,

Matt. 18: 8, it is better for thee to enter into life lame or maimed, than having two hands to be cast *into eternal fire,* εἰς τὸ πῦρ τὸ αἰώνιον.

Matt. 25: 41, depart from me, ye cursed, *into everlasting fire,* εἰς τὸ πῦρ τὸ αἰώνιον.

Matt. 25; 46, these shall go away into *everlasting punishment,* εἰς κόλασιν αἰώνιον, [but the righteous *into everlasting life,* εἰς ζωὴν αἰώνιον.]

Mark 3: 29, whoever shall utter blasphemy against the Holy Spirit, shall never obtain forgiveness, but be obnoxious to *eternal condemnation,* αἰωνίου κρίσεως.

2 Thess. 1: 9, who shall be punished with *everlasting destruction* from the presence of the Lord, ὄλεθρον αἰώνιον.

Heb. 6: 2, not again imparting elementary instruction with respect to repentance . . . and *eternal judgement,* i. e. eternal condemnation or punishment, αἰωνίου κρίσεως.

Jude v. 6, suffering the punishment *of eternal fire,* πυρὸς αἰωνίου.

I leave these cases without remark for the present, reserving my conclusions until I have made some additional remarks.

§ 13. General Summary of the meanings of Αἰώνιος.

It appears from the above representation, that there are 66 cases in which αἰώνιος is employed in the New Testament. Of these, 51 are used in relation to the happiness of the righteous; 2, in relation to God or to his glory; 6 are of a miscellaneous nature, but the meaning of αἰώνιος in them all is quite clear; and 7 relate to the subject of future punishment.

In regard to all the cases of αἰώνιος, which have a relation to *future* time, it is quite plain and certain, that they designate *an endless period, an unlimited duration*. I except of course, for the present, those 7 cases which have respect to future punishment. But in regard to the rest, if they have not the meaning which has just been stated, then the Scriptures do not decide that God is eternal, nor that the happiness of the righteous is without end; nor that his covenant of grace will always remain; a conclusion which would forever blast the hopes of Christians, and shroud in more than midnight darkness all the glories of the gospel.

The above are all the instances in which αἰώνιος is employed in the New Testament; with the exception of 1 Tim. 6: 19, where the reading cannot be satisfactorily defended. I purposely avoid all readings of this nature, in the present investigation.

In seeking for all the examples of αἰών and αἰώνιος, in the New Testament, I have used the Concordance of Schmidt, which, having been published before the critical investigations of the Greek were made, may possibly

§§ 13. 14. *Summary of the meanings of Αἰώνιος.* 47

contain some two or three instances less of these words, than are to be found in the Greek text of Dr. Knapp, which is the one that I have used. If it should prove to be so ; or that I have overlooked some one instance, in such a minute and protracted examination ; it will not have any effect on the reasoning or state of evidence at large, in regard to the subject before us. I trust, moreover, that it will not be imputed to any design on my part.

The reader has now before him, a full view of the manner in which the sacred writers of the New Testament employ the words αἰών and αἰώνιος. We might next proceed, therefore, to draw some conclusion, by comparing the whole together, and in this way shewing in what sense the sacred writers probably applied these words to the *future punishment* of the wicked. But I must beg the reader to delay a while longer, in order that we may obtain a fuller view of facts relating to the usage of these same words by the Septuagint translators, and of the corresponding Hebrew word עוֹלָם. I shall be as brief as possible here ; not considering it necessary to produce more than a few citations, as examples in proof of what may be stated. The *direct* evidence I have fully stated ; the *indirect*, I may be indulged the liberty of producing in a briefer and more summary way.

---

§ 14. *Meaning of* עוֹלָם *in the Hebrew of the Old Testament.*

This is, (1) *Eternity, unlimited duration.*

So Gesenius, in the recent edition (the third) of his Hebrew Lexicon, " עוֹלָם, *eternity ;*" which is the only

§ 14. *Meaning of* עוֹלָם.

definition that he gives. He goes on however to say, that "the expression in Hebrew, as among us in common life, is often used in an inaccurate manner, i. e. when merely a very long space of time is denoted." Of this, more in the sequel.

I would remark here, for the sake of brevity, that the words in the quotations which follow, that are printed in Italic, correspond to the Hebrew word עוֹלָם, in some one of its forms. After this explanation I shall not repeat the Hebrew word, but only quote the English.

Gen. 9: 16, that I may remember the *everlasting* covenant.

Gen. 17: 7, I will establish my covenant . . . . for an *everlasting* covenant.

Gen. 17: 13, my covenant shall be . . . an *everlasting* covenant. The same in Gen. 17: 19.

Gen. 21: 33, Abraham . . . . called on the name of Jehovah, the *everlasting* God.

Deut. 33: 27, the *eternal* God is thy refuge.

Ps. 90: 2, *from everlasting to everlasting*, thou art God.

Ps. 103: 17, the mercy of the Lord is *from everlasting to everlasting*.

Ps. 112: 6, the righteous shall be in *everlasting* remembrance.

Prov. 10: 25, the righteous is an *everlasting* foundation.

Is. 35: 10, the ransomed of the Lord shall return and come to Zion, with songs and *everlasting* joy upon their heads.

Is. 40: 28, the *everlasting* God.

Is. 51: 11, the redeemed of the Lord shall return . . . and *everlasting* joy shall be upon their head.

§ 14. *Meaning of* עוֹלָם.

Is. 56: 5, I will give them an *everlasting* name, that shall not be cut off.

Is. 60: 19, Jehovah shall be thine *everlasting* light. The same again in 60: 20.

Is. 61: 7, *everlasting* joy shall be to them.

Is. 63: 12, to make himself an *everlasting* name.

Jer. 10: 10, the living God [is] an *everlasting* king.

Jer. 31: 3, I have loved thee with an *everlasting* love.

Dan. 12: 2, some [shall awake] to *everlasting* life; and some, to shame and *everlasting* contempt.

These are only a small proportion of the cases which might easily be produced; but these are enough to shew what meaning עוֹלָם usually bears, in the Hebrew Scriptures.

As a confirmation of this, I will add a few cases where the phrase לְעוֹלָם , עַד עוֹלָם etc. are employed, which correspond to εἰς τὸν αἰῶνα, εἰς αἰῶνα, εἰς τοὺς αἰῶνας, etc., in the Septuagint and in the New Testament.

Ex. 14: 13, ye shall see them [the Egyptians], no more *forever*.

Deut. 12: 28, that it may be well with thee, and thy children after thee *forever*.

1 Sam. 20: 15, thou shalt not cut off thy kindness from my house *forever*.

2 Sam. 3: 28, we are guiltless . . . . *forever*.

Ps. 89: 4, thy seed will I establish *forever*.

Ps. 131: 3, let Israel hope in the Lord *forever*.

Ps. 136 exhibits 26 instances, where the same sense is certain in them all.

Under the form לְעוֹלָם (εἰς αἰῶνα) alone, in the sense of *forever*, Taylor in his Hebrew Concordance, has arranged some 175 instances. If we add to these, all the various forms of עוֹלָם , to which the meaning, *forever*,

§ 14. *Meaning of* עוֹלָם.

always, time unlimited, or *without end*, is clearly to be attributed, several hundreds more must be added to the 175 cases. It is impossible to doubt, in regard to the *usual* meaning of the word עוֹלָם in the Hebrew Scriptures. But then,

(2) As Gesenius remarks, עוֹלָם is sometimes applied (as in common life) to things which endure for a *long time, for an indefinite period*. So it is applied to the Jewish priesthood; to the Mosaic ordinances; to the possession of the land of Canaan; to the hills and mountains; to the earth; to the time of service to be rendered by a slave; and to some other things of a like nature. But all the instances of such a nature, taken collectively, amount to a very small proportion of the whole, and can in no way be looked upon as any thing more than a kind of exception to predominant, plain, certain usage.

In our own language, (where *eternal* and *everlasting* surely designate *a period without end*) we often employ the same words to designate *that which seems to have no end*, or *the end of which is not defined* or *seen*. Thus we say, *everlasting talker, perpetual scourge, eternal vexation, endless trouble, everlasting disquiet*, etc.; all employed, in common parlance, for that which endures a great while, or for an indefinite period, or which is without intermission. Yet who supposes, that on this account the words *everlasting, eternal, perpetual, endless*, are not, with the strictest propriety, applied to *time which has no bounds*, or in other words, to *eternity?*

Thus much then for the Hebrew word עוֹלָם, when it relates to *future time*. It is very clear, that when Gesenius defines it *Ewigkeit* [eternity], he rightly defines it. This is its sense, in an overwhelming predominance

§ 14. *Meaning of* עוֹלָם.

of examples. All the meanings derived from this, are only exceptions, and amount to mere examples of *catachrestic* usage, i. e. usage which is uncommon, or aside from the strict sense of the word. Such is the usage in all languages, with regard to more or less of important words.

(3) In respect to עוֹלָם, as applied to designate *time past*, it has the same shades of meaning with the Greek αἰών, αἰώνιος, as explained in pp. 24 and 44 seq. This usage is not very frequent, when compared with the designation of *time future*. Still, there are, in the whole, a considerable number of instances; enough clearly to exhibit the *usus loquendi* in this respect. Any one may easily find them, by consulting his Concordance. A number of these I will here subjoin, to illustrate the usage in question.

Is. 63: 9, 11. Job 22: 15. Ps. 143: 3. Prov. 23: 10. Is. 42: 14. Mic. 5: 2. Prov. 22: 28. Jer. 18: 15. Ezek. 36: 2. 26: 20. Ps. 93: 2. 103: 17. 77: 5.

§ 15. *General Summary in regard to* עוֹלָם.

From what has been exhibited in regard to עוֹלָם, it is plain, that it corresponds throughout with the Greek αἰών and αἰώνιος of the New Testament, when employed in their *primary* sense, viz. as having reference to *time*, either *future* or *past*. Of this agreement, we shall soon have occasion to take further notice.

But in regard to the secondary class of meanings which αἰών bears in the New Testament, viz. that of *world* with the various adsignifications noticed above; there is no case in the Old Testament Hebrew in which

§ 15. *Summary of the meanings of* עוֹלָם.

עוֹלָם bears this sense, if we except Ecc. 3: 11 which is too doubtful to build upon. Putting, therefore, this class of meanings out of the account, (all of which are deduced from the meaning affixed to עוֹלָם after the Old Testament Scriptures were completed, i. e. by the later Hebrews), the coincidence between αἰών and עוֹלָם is very striking; so much so, that nothing can be more evident, than that the one corresponds with the other in most cases throughout, and that each reflects light upon the other. He who thoroughly understands the use of עוֹלָם, is better prepared to understand the meanings of αἰών· and he who has a complete knowledge of the use of αἰών, is well qualified to understand the use of עוֹלָם.

One point only of difference worthy of remark, do I find. This is, that it so happens in regard to the use of αἰών in the New Testament, that it is applied in no case to designate simply a period of time which has *definite limitations;* I mean such limitations as from the nature of the case must be regarded as definite, and as known to be so. For example; in the Old Testament עוֹלָם is applied to the Jewish ordinances, priesthood, and kingly succession; to the hills, mountains, and world; to the possession of the land of Canaan, etc. But in the New Testament, no instances of a use so *catachrestic* as this occur. An *indefinite, unlimited period,* is the basis of all the significations of αἰών and αἰώνιος there, wherever they have a simple reference to *time.* At most, we can only except some few cases, where the reference is to *past,* and not to *future* time.

The distinctive trait of usage in the New Testament which has now been pointed out, deserves consideration, and ought to have its proper weight, in determining the signification of the words in question by the *usus loquendi* of the New Testament writers.

§ 16. *Use of αἰών and αἰώνιος in the Septuagint.*

If I have counted rightly, *αἰών*, in some of its forms, is employed in the Septuagint version of the Old Testament 308 times; all as translations of עוֹלָם, in some one of its forms. Of these, 184 instances correspond to לְעוֹלָם in the Hebrew; and 71, to עַד עוֹלָם its equivalent. In almost the whole of these instances in which *αἰών* is employed, the signification of *time unlimited, a period without end*, is, beyond all reasonable question, absolutely certain; just as it is with respect to the Hebrew words, to which *αἰών* corresponds. In the great number of instances in which *αἰών* is employed in the Septuagint, some cases occur of its *catachrestic* use; precisely in the same manner as of the Hebrew word עוֹלָם, which has already been noted above, p. 59. In short, the most unpractised observer as to the phenomena of language, cannot help remarking that *αἰών* is, throughout the Old Testament, the word corresponding to עוֹלָם, which the Seventy have *almost uniformly* appropriated to this purpose. Nothing can be clearer, than that they considered it as the *equivalent* of עוֹלָם. So much is this actually the case, that I have been able to find only about 20 cases, in the whole, where the word *αἰών* is employed by them, unless it be as the translation of עוֹלָם. Most of these cases, also, plainly relate to expressions in Hebrew which are equivalent to עוֹלָם, viz. such as לָנֶצַח, עַד, עֲדֵי עַד, and לָעַד. The few other cases which exist, plainly result from a reading in the text of the Septuagint translators, different from that in our present Hebrew Bibles.

In regard to *αἰώνιος*, I find 92 instances, in which the Septuagint has employed it. In six of these, it cor-

§ 16. *Αἰών and Αἰώνιος in the Septuagint.*

responds to other words than עוֹלָם; in all the rest, to some form of this word.

In respect to the meaning of *αἰώνιος*, it is perfectly obvious that the great body of the cases in which it is employed, will admit of no other meaning than that of *eternal, everlasting*. But there are a few cases, in which the *catachrestic* use of it must be admitted. Thus the mountains, the Levitical statutes, priesthood, rites, covenant, also landmarks, waste-places, etc. are called *αἰώνιοι*, precisely in the same manner as עוֹלָם is sometimes applied in the Old Testament, and corresponding throughout with it. The word *αἰώνιος*, therefore, is, in the Septuagint, less strictly applied to *indefinite time, an unlimited period*, than it is in the New Testament. Just the same is the case with *αἰών*, as we have already seen.

I refrain from pursuing my inquiries through the Apocryphal books; from which a great copiousness of examples might also be adduced, to confirm the views which have already been given of the meaning of *αἰών* and *αἰώνιος*. It is quite superfluous to pursue the investigation any further. We have critical materials enough before us to make up a decision, if such materials can ever avail for this purpose.

§ 17. *Bearing of the testimony on the subject of future punishment.*

We have now surveyed the use of the words *αἰών* and *αἰώνιος* in the whole latitude of their Scriptural use; and we come, at the close, with all the views before us which this investigation and discussion have afforded, to see if we can form a satisfactory judgement as to the meaning

§ 17. *Bearing of the testimony, etc.*

of the words in question, when applied to designate the period of *future punishment.*

Let us first lay aside all those various meanings of αἰών and αἰώνιος, which cannot have any direct bearing on the great question before us. Of this class, plainly, are all those in which αἰών has the *secondary* meaning of *world;* some few peculiar ones only excepted, which I shall hereafter notice.

Of the same class, too, are all those meanings of αἰών and αἰώνιος which have relation to *time past.*

It is plain, moreover, that inasmuch as *future* punishment must belong to *future* time, so αἰών, when connected with the designation of such punishment, must, (if the laws of universal analogy in philology and exegesis are to be observed), have a like meaning with that which it has, when applied to other things belonging to a future world, and which are yet to take place.

In all the cases where glory and praise are ascribed to God *forever*, or *forever* and *ever*, it will not be credited that the sacred writers mean to declare, that this will take place for *only a definite period of time*, or *for certain ages only.* It will not be doubted, that when God is called *eternal*, αἰώνιος; or when the things of the heavenly world are said to be so; that *eternity* in the proper sense of the word is meant.

I trust it will not be questioned, in regard to the 9 cases where αἰών is *applied to the happiness of the righteous* in another world, and the 51 cases where αἰώνιος is applied to the same, that a happiness *without limits, without end,* is intended to be designated. For all these cases, which I shall not repeat here, I must refer the reader to pp. 19. 40 above, where he will see them produced at full length.

§ 17. *Bearing of the testimony*

Can it be reasonably doubted, then, that the 15 cases in which αἰών is applied to the *future punishment* of the wicked, and the 7 cases in which αἰώνιος is applied to the same subject, have a meaning like that of the preceding cases? The time designated in both is *future;* the world is *future.* The intention of the writers seems very apparently to have been similar in both cases. The invariable laws of interpretation, therefore, would seem to demand a like exegesis.

Let us for a moment, examine this last position.

I take it to be a rule of construing all *antithetic* forms of expression, that where you can perceive the force of one side of the antithesis, you do of course come to a knowledge of the force of the other side. If *life eternal* is promised on one side, and *death eternal* is threatened on the other and opposite one, is it not to be supposed, that the word *eternal* which qualifies *death*, is a word of equal force and import with the word *eternal* which qualifies *life?* In no other case could a doubt be raised, with regard to such a principle. I venture to say that the exception here, (if such an one must be made), is without any parallel in the just principles of interpretation.

If then the words αἰών and αἰώνιος are applied 60 times (which is the fact) in the New Testament, to designate the *continuance* of the future happiness of the righteous; and some 12 times to designate the *continuance* of the future misery of the wicked; by what principles of interpreting language does it become possible for us, to avoid the conclusion that αἰών and αἰώνιος have the same sense in both cases?

Will it be said, that we must appeal to arguments here deduced from the light of nature, in order to determine the probable meaning of αἰών and αἰώνιος, when connected with the future punishment of the wicked? But how can we do this? The light of nature at best, as we have before seen, merely renders it probable in some degree that the soul may always exist. Does it—can it—determine, then, what is to be its condition; and how long this is to continue? It is impossible. Or if we insist still on what the light of nature can do, then let us go to those who enjoyed it, and see how they decided in relation to the question before us. Did not the Greeks and Romans hold to the *eternity* of future punishments? Notoriously they did. And could we, with such light merely as they had, come to an *opposite* conclusion?

But if the declaration of the Scriptures is to be our guide, in regard to our creed on this point; and if we are to ask simply what the Bible declares, and not what in our view it ought to declare; then must this great question, like every other one in *revealed* theology, be ultimately settled by an appeal to the nature, power, and laws of language. Such an appeal I have endeavoured to make; and the result is what I have expressed above.

It does most plainly and indubitably follow, that *if the Scriptures have not asserted the* ENDLESS *punishment of the wicked, neither have they asserted the* ENDLESS *happiness of the righteous, nor the* ENDLESS *glory and existence of the Godhead.* The one is equally certain with the other. Both are laid in the same balance. They must be tried by the same tests. And if we give up the one, we must, in order to be consistent, give up the other also.

But if the eternity of God's glory, attributes, and existence, if the eternity of future happiness, are to be given up as *revealed* doctrines; on what basis are these doctrines to be placed? How are we entitled any longer to receive them as true, and to hold fast to them as certain?

Tell me not of *the light of nature* here. I must believe, (I trust there are very many others who will feel constrained with me to believe), that *the* GOSPEL *has brought life and immortality to light,* and that no mere "son of nature" "hath seen God at any time;" "but that the only-begotten, who is in the bosom of the Father, he hath revealed him." Believing this—fully believing this—I must feel, that the criticism which would decide against the *endless* punishment of the wicked, must also, to be consistent, blast my hopes of eternal life, and cover the glories of the Godhead with everlasting darkness.

I feel constrained, moreover, to ask here, If αἰών and αἰώνιος do not signify *eternity* and *eternal,* in the Greek language of the Septuagint and New Testament, then what terms has this language to express such an idea? Will any one venture to say, that the sacred writers had no such idea as *eternity* and *eternal?* If he will, I do not think him worthy of refutation. But if it be admitted that the idea in question was familiar to them, then by what terms could they express it in the Greek language, so appropriate as those which have now been examined?

I admit that a Greek could convey the idea of *eternity* and *eternal,* in a variety of ways, by different modes of expression; just as we can in English, or as a Hebrew could in his language. It is true, moreover, that the New Testament writers, and the Septuagint, have conveyed the ideas in question, occasionally, by the use of other words, and by peculiar phrases. But after all, the essence of the difficulty remains. The question is substantially unanswered by these considerations. It cannot be shewn, that any words are *so appropriate* to the object named, as the words αἰών and αἰώνιος.

Still clearer if possible is it, that the proper word in Hebrew for *eternity*, is עוֹלָם; to which, in so many hundred instances, αἰών and αἰώνιος clearly correspond.

Must not every philologist and every serious inquirer feel, then, that *conjecture* is out of question, in regard to determining such a case as that before us? The meaning of such words is not to be *guessed at;* but to be made out by analogy, and by a regular and impartial application of the laws of language.

I admit the awful nature of the conclusion, that the punishment of a future world is to have no end. I do most fully admit, that it is indeed " a fearful thing to fall into the hands of the living God." But what if I should doubt or deny it? Can this have any influence on that eternal Judge, who will pronounce my final sentence? None. Can my denial of what he has said, or my refusal to explain it in analogy with all his other declarations relative to things of the future world, or my efforts to fritter away the meaning of his declarations—can all this avail me, when I stand an unembodied, naked, helpless spirit before his searching eye, and the tribunal of his almighty power? O the dreadful thought! What if I deceive myself, and cry out, *" peace! peace!"* while my God saith, " There is no peace to the wicked?" Will this repeal his law, alter its meaning, or frustrate its penalty? It is indeed a fearful hazard, for men to cast themselves for safety on such a desperate wreck as this!

If there be any relief for the dark prospects of the wicked as to the future, it must come only from this source, viz. that the Bible has disclosed some method of *future* relief, some encouragement that *future* reformation and penitence will restore the lost favour of God. But alas! where is this to be found? On this subject of unspeakable and everlasting moment, of tremendous interest, there is not one assertion—one word even—in all the book of God, which, when construed by the usual laws of language, can afford a gleam of hope. Where is another state of probation described? What are the means of grace to be enjoyed in *Hell?* Is it the preaching of the gospel? Is it the influence of the Spirit of God? Who *preaches*, in the bottomless pit; or how shall the Spirit of God dwell with blasphemers and reprobates?

Will *misery* of itself make men penitent? And this, in a world from which the means of grace are excluded? All, all makes against such a supposition. There is not a sentence in the Scriptures which asserts it, or even gives any countenance to it. All the warnings and exhortations which the Scriptures contain, go upon the ground of men's *present* state of trial being their *final* and *decisive* one. It is impossible to believe rationally, that men of such benevolence as were the writers of the holy Scriptures, should not have told us something about a *future* probation and acceptance, if these were known to them. If they have not told us of these, then, it is because they did not believe in them, they did not know any thing of them. And if they did not, how can we venture to believe that we have any knowledge of them?

On this point, I acknowledge my convictions are strong. I have long searched, with anxious solicitude, for a text in the Bible which would even seem to favour the idea of a *future* probation. I cannot find it. If others have been more successful in their researches, let them shew us the proof of it. When this shall be done, in accordance with the simple laws of interpretation, and without the application of *a priori* theology to the Bible, then I promise to renounce my feelings and views in regard to the whole subject before me.

Until then, I must hold to the *endless* punishment of the wicked, or give up the *endless* happiness of the righteous. And if the hope of this must be abandoned, then may we well ask, what the gospel has revealed that is worth our knowing; or of what value is the existence which the Creator has given us?

I take it for granted, that all my readers will understand, that the evidence in respect to future punishment, derived from the use of $αἰών$ and $αἰώνιος$, is only a part —a moderate part—of what the Scriptures contain relative to this subject. My design, in the present inquiry, is not to present *at large* the subject of future punishment. To produce *all* the arguments, and examine *all* the objections, would require a book instead of a short essay; and years of study, instead of a few days.

§ 18. *Results.*

Thus have I endeavoured to present, as briefly as my plan would permit, the result of a philological and exegetical examination of the words $αἰών$ and $αἰώνιος$, as employed by the writers of the New Testament. I may have performed a work superfluous for some of my readers; who perhaps have elsewhere found what has better satisfied their minds, than that which has now been laid before them. But if there be any critical and hermeneutical essay of this nature, which goes the full length of the subject, it is unknown to me; and I have merely followed my own plan in the above researches, and made all my investigations, without the aid of any lexicons or commentators. My reason for this has not been, an aim to be *original;* much less, a disregard to the opinions of others. It has been simply this, viz. a desire not to embarrass my mind with any *previous* opinions or views. I wished to form my conclusion merely from the word of God, investigated with diligence and care, and in a manner as unembarrassed as it was possible for me to adopt, in my circumstances.

The result seems to me to be plain, and philologically and exegetically certain. It is this ; either the declarations of the Scriptures do not establish the facts, that God and his glory and praise and happiness are *endless ;* nor that the happiness of the righteous in a future world, is *endless ;* or else they establish the fact, that the punishment of the wicked is *endless.* The whole stand or fall together. There can, from the very nature of antithesis, be no room for rational doubt here, in what manner we should interpret the declarations of the sacred writers. WE MUST EITHER ADMIT THE ENDLESS MISERY OF HELL, OR GIVE UP THE ENDLESS HAPPINESS OF HEAVEN.

§ 19. *Manner in which the words αἰών and αἰώνιος have been treated by some critics and lexicographers.*

As a kind of supplement to the above investigation, and for the sake of communicating a fuller view of the words in question than most of my readers may readily find, I must beg the liberty of adding, by way of Appendix, a few strictures on the manner in which Lexicographers and others have treated αἰών and αἰώνιος. It is high time that these words were accurately understood,

§ 19. *Αἰών* and *Αἰώνιος* in the Lexicons.

and handled in a manner truly philological. If what I have said, or may say, will contribute toward the accomplishment of so important an object; or at least excite others to do what needs to be done; my labour will not be in vain. Such of my readers as pursue the critical study of the Scriptures, will probably not be uninterested in the remarks which follow. Others may omit the reading of them, should they find them to be destitute of special interest to their own minds.

In regard to the Lexicons, I shall be brief. I perceive, on an examination of Schleusner, that my arrangement differs in some respects from his. I will not delay here for the purpose of controverting his arrangement, but only to make a few remarks on some parts of it. I must leave the rest to the judgement of every reader, who will take the pains to examine this author.

The first meaning which he gives to *αἰών*, is, *a definite and long time*, i. e. a long continued, but still a *definite* period of time. Under this head he arranges Matt. 21: 19, which is the case of the fig-tree that was cursed. Now the Saviour is represented by the evangelists as saying, 'Let there be no more fruit from thee *εἰς τὸν αἰῶνα, forever*;' which surely does not imply, that the time would come to an *end* in which this tree would be barren, or after which it would again bear fruit. In other words, *definite* time is clearly *not* marked here.

Again, he puts John 8: 35 under the same head; 'the servant does *not* abide in the house *forever,*' *οὐ* . . . . *εἰς τὸν αἰῶνα*, but the Son abideth *forever, εἰς τὸν αἰῶνα*. Can this mean, in either case, a *definite* period of time?

His second head is, *life of man, age of man*, or *time during which he lives*.

As an example of this, he appeals to Matt. 12: 32;

§ 19. *Αἰών* and *Αἰώνιος* in the Lexicons.

'They shall not obtain forgiveness, neither *in this world*, ἐν τούτῳ τῷ αἰῶνι·' which he renders, *neither in this life*, i. e. in this age of man. But on this ground, what does αἰών mean in the antithesis, viz., οὔτε ἐν τῷ μέλλοντι [αἰῶνι], *nor in the life to come?* If a *definite* period is simply meant in the first part of this antithesis, what is the *definite* period of the life to come? In other words, When will it cease? This incongruity is avoided, when the sense of *world* is given to αἰών in each case. Both expressions together then make out an *intensive* affirmation, equivalent to *never, never.*

Schleusner also appeals to Matt. 28: 20, in confirmation of the sense which he here gives to αἰών. 'Lo I am with you always even to the end of the world,' ἕως τῆς συντελείας τοῦ αἰῶνος· (in which however, he has omitted to insert *always,* πάσας τὰς ἡμέρας). This he construes as meaning simply, 'I am with you to the end of your lives;' thus making the whole promise attach only to the apostles. I cannot persuade myself that this was the meaning of Christ, or the only tenor of this promise.

He then arranges the meaning of αἰών under, (3) *Men of any age.* (4) *External things of the present life, riches, pleasures,* etc. (5) *Method of living, genius of the age, manners of the age.* (6) *Vicious men of any age.* *After* all these, comes the meaning on which the whole of them turned, viz. (7) *World, universe.* He comes only in No. 9, to the meaning of *eternity, unlimited period.*

How incongruous this arrangement is with the meaning of the word αἰών as used in the New Testament or the Old, must be apparent from the preceding exhibitions of this word which have been made. How loose and indefinite some of the meanings here given are, and how

§ 19. *Αἰών* and *Αἰώνιος* in the Lexicons. 65

far deflected from the original significations of *αἰών* and *αἰώνιος*, even in the Old Testament; must be very apparent even to an unpractised observer. Indeed, it is plain that the Hebrew usage of עוֹלָם, as distinguished into the *ancient* and *modern*, did not once occur to Schleusner, in its proper form; and of course, he has failed to do justice to the corresponding *αἰών*.

On the whole, I must consider the article *αἰών* in his Lexicon, as one of the unfortunate specimens of imperfect lexicography, which now and then occur in this venerable, and (in general) truly valuable writer.

The Lexicon of Wahl, in regard to this word as well as very many others, affords a far better specimen of skill, neatness, and accuracy of arrangement. Wahl has arranged thus; (1) *Time, unlimited duration, aevum.* (2) *The universe, mundus.* (3) *An age, period of the world;* under which he arranges, (*a*) *The present age,* i. e. the Jewish age or period antecedent to the Messiah. Under this head he arranges the following senses, viz. (1) Simply, *age.* (2) *Age,* with the accessory idea of *vitiosity, imbecility,* etc. (*b*) *The future age,* i. e. the reign of the Messiah, a period of happiness, liberty, piety, etc.

This is indeed a great amendment of Schleusner's mistaken, unphilological, and (I had almost said) unaccountable arrangement. But this exhibits some important mistakes, which, (unless I am greatly in error), are adapted to mislead the student of the original Scriptures, who places too much confidence in lexicographal guides.

Under No. 2, he arranges the signification, *universe, mundus.* I had myself, before I gave עוֹלָם and *αἰών* an extended and minute investigation, been accustomed to suppose, that *αἰῶνες* in 1 Tim. 1: 17. Heb. 1: 2. 11: 3, must mean the *universe;* particularly, because the *plural*

§ 19. *Αἰών and Αἰώνιος in the Lexicons.*

number is here employed. It was doubtless on the like account, that Wahl also gave to αἰῶνες the same signification. But a minute inquiry into the grounds of such a rendering, has convinced me of my own mistake; and of course, that Wahl is also in an error.

In recurring back to the ancient Hebrew usage of עוֹלָם, I observe that there is no apparent difference between the use of the *plural* number, and the *singular*, in order to designate *time*. So 1 Kings 8: 13, a settled place . . . . to abide in *for ever*, עוֹלָמִים. See also, for the like examples, 2 Chron. 6: 2. Ps. 61: 5 (4). Ps. 77: 6 (5), where עוֹלָמִים has the sense of *ancient times*. Ps. 145: 13, (*everlasting*). Is. 26: 4. 45: 17. Dan. 9: 24. Is. 51: 9, (*ancient*). Ecc. 1: 10. (id.) Ps. 77: 8 *(for ever)*. Is. 45: 17, עוֹלְמֵי עַד, *ages of perpetuity, for ever and ever.*

These instances make it clear, that the plural is used in the same sense as the singular, or at least without any assignable difference of meaning. If there be any difference at all, it must consist merely in this, viz. that the plural number is a somewhat more *intensive* form of expression than the singular. But although this is often the case in Hebrew, yet in the present case, the nature of the several instances where the singular and plural are used being compared and well considered, it will be plainly seen, that there is no ground for making any assignable difference of meaning between the different numbers.

In just the same way the Seventy have employed αἰών. Sometimes they have rendered the *plural* of עוֹלָם, by the singular αἰών, e. g. Dan. 5: 10, let the king reign לְעָלְמִין (Chaldee), εἰς τὸν αἰῶνα. So Is. 47: 17, they shall not be ashamed עַד עוֹלְמֵי עַד, Septuagint ἕως τοῦ

§ 19. *Aἰών* and *Aἰώνιος* in the Lexicons. 67

αἰῶνος ἔτι. In the same verse, עוֹלָמִים is translated by αἰώνιον. In like manner Is. 51: 9, דֹּרוֹת עוֹלָמִים is rendered γενεὰ αἰῶνος. So Ps. 90: 8, עֲלֻמֵנוּ, *our secret* [sins], plural number; but the Seventy, reading it עֲלָמֵנוּ, have rendered it ὁ αἰὼν ἡμῶν, Ps. 89: 8. By a like mistake in reading, they have again rendered עֲוִילִים, *little children*, in Job 19: 18, by εἰς τὸν αἰῶνα, because they read it עוֹלָמִים.

On the other hand, the Seventy have used the *plural* of αἰών, in order to translate the *singular* of some words which are equivalent to עוֹלָם; e. g. קֶדֶם in Ps. 55: 20, is rendered πρὸ τῶν αἰώνων by the Septuagint, Ps. 54: 19.

So also the *plural* form of עוֹלָם is often used in the Hebrew, as equivalent to the singular, i. e. as having the same meaning; e. g. 1 K. 8: 13. 2 Chron. 6: 2. Ps. 61: 5. 77: 6. Dan. 2: 4 (Chaldee). 3: 9. 6: 22, and so frequently.

I have only to add, that a comparison of usage in the New Testament, will lead to the same result with regard to αἰών.

So far then as it respects the designation of *time*, the singular and plural of *αἰών* answer the same purpose. But is this the case, in regard to the use of *αἰών* in the *secondary* and *later* sense of עוֹלָם, viz. that of *world*, etc. ?

If we go back to Hebrew usage, we shall find no example in it to justify the use of the *plural* number in the sense of *worlds*; i. e. in such a sense as astronomy has taught us of the present day to employ this plural word. In the old Hebrew, אֶרֶץ means *earth;* but the plural אֲרָצוֹת, means *lands* only in the sense of *countries*, not in the sense of *worlds*. The other appellation for *world* is תֵּבֵל, which is employed only in poetry. This has no plural.

§ 19. Αἰών and Αἰώνιος in the Lexicons.

When the Hebrew wanted to designate the *heavenly bodies*, he said, *host of heaven*, צְבָא הַשָּׁמַיִם; or כּוֹכָבִים, *stars*; or sun, moon, and stars; or שָׁמַיִם *heavens*, simply. There is no intimation in the Scriptures, as I can find, that there is more than one *world*.

Hence I must take αἰῶνες in 1 Tim. 1: 17. Heb. 1: 2. 11: 3, to mean *world* simply, i. e. our world, this earth. And if it be asked, Whether the Scriptures do not ascribe any thing more than the creation of our world to the Son of God ? the answer is given in Heb. 1: 10, ' Thou, Lord, didst lay the foundations of the earth, and the *heavens* are the work of thy hands.' The same sentiment also may be found in Col. 1: 16. Eph. 3: 9. John 1: 3, and in other passages.

That the plural and singular of nouns are often employed in the same manner, and to designate one and the same thing, no tyro in sacred philology can fail to know. For example, in Hebrew ; מִשְׁכָּן *dwelling*, מִשְׁכָּנִים *dwelling*; אֵל *God*, אֱלֹהִים *God*; יָם *sea*, יַמִּים *sea*; חָכְמָה *wisdom*, חָכְמוֹת *wisdom*; יָשָׁר *the upright*, יְשָׁרִים *the upright*; רָשָׁע *the wicked*, רְשָׁעִים *the wicked*; תְּהוֹם *the abyss*, תְּהֹמוֹת *the abyss*. So in Hebrew Greek ; σάββατον *the sabbath*, σάββατα the same ; οὐρανός *the heavens*, οὐρανοί the same, etc.

There is nothing at all peculiar, then, in using αἰῶνες in the same sense as αἰών, or in employing either of them indifferently, to designate the idea of *world* in the singular number.

I should not have said thus much on the error in the Lexicons with regard to the *plural* of this word, had I not seen much reasoning about the meaning of *ages of ages* (αἰῶνες αἰώνων), that is built on a supposed distinction of meaning between the singular and plural number.

§ 19. *Aἰών* and *Aἰώνιος* in the Lexicons.

Many writers would seem to ask, 'What can *ages of ages* mean, unless *age* (*αἰών*) is a *definite, limited period?* Of course, must not *ages of ages*, after all, be only a series of *limited* periods, and finally have a *termination?*'

The answer to this is not difficult. In regard to the plural number *αἰῶνες*, it imports of itself no more than the singular. In regard to the form of expression *ages of ages*, or *age of ages*, or *age of age*, (for all these are indifferently employed), it is a mere *intensive* form of expression, and nothing more nor less. What are *servant of servants, lord of lords, holy of holies, heaven of heavens,* etc., but *intensive* forms of expression? And if any one should ask, Whether any thing can be added to the idea of *eternity*, of *unlimited duration?* in order to shew that there is an incongruity in employing *αἰών*, in the expressions now before us, with an *unlimited* sense; I would reply by asking, Whether *forever* in English does not mean *eternity, unlimited duration?* If so, then how can we *add* to it? Yet we do say, *forever* and *ever;* that is, we do use an *intensive* expression, in order to designate with emphasis the idea of a *never-ending* period of time. Could not the Hebrew, then, say לְעוֹלָם וָעֶד; and the Greek, *εἰς τοὺς αἰῶνας τῶν αἰώνων*, in the very same sense, and for the very same purpose, as we say *forever and ever?*

He could; he did: and all criticisms on these phrases, which would deduce any thing more from them than *intensiveness* of expression, is built on an imaginary basis, not on one which has its support in the *usus loquendi* of either the Greek, Hebrew, or English language.

There is another mistake, (as it seems to me), in Wahl's article on *αἰών*. He has, throughout, made *present* world etc., and *world to come* etc., mean, the age preceding the Messiah, and the age after his advent. In doing this, he has appealed to the Jewish usage of *this world*, and *the world to come*, עוֹלָם הַזֶּה and עוֹלָם הַבָּא. But this appeal is very far from sustaining him. The Rabbinical Jews divided *this world* into *the lower world*, i. e. the proper earth with all that it contains; *the middle world*, i. e. the region of the air, including the heavenly bodies; and *the supreme* or *upper world*, i. e. the world of angels, etc.

In regard to *world to come* or *future world*, some held it to be the *new* world, which would arise after the destruction of the present; others, (and this I take to be the general usage), held it to be the world of souls, i. e. the future world in the same sense in which we now use this phrase in English; *some* only, (Buxtorf merely says *quidam*), regarded it as meaning *the days* or *age of the Messiah*. Could any one justly expect such a train of deduction from this, as appears in the Lexicon of Wahl?

Of all the numerous cases, which he arranges under the head of *age before and after the Messiah*, not more than three will stand the test of investigation; viz. 1 Cor. 10: 11. Eph. 2: 7. Heb. 6: 5. Of these, Eph. 2: 7 is by no means necessarily arranged under the head in question, as it may easily be understood simply of *ages to come*, and more probably should be so understood.

As to the other cases, where *the present* αἰών and the αἰών *to come*, are expressed or implied, I take nothing to be more certain, than that the arrangement of Wahl is fundamentally erroneous. It is not only without any basis in predominant Jewish usage; but it would force on the text of the New Testament a sense strange enough in some cases, and unnecessary in all.

When our Saviour, in the parable of the sower, says,

§ 19. *Αἰών* and *Αἰώνιος* in the Lexicons. 71

'The cares *of this world;*' is there any special relation here to the *age which preceded the Messiah?* Was there then to be no *world* in the sense here plainly meant, *after* the Messiah had come? Rather, does not the whole parable represent all the occurrencies to which it alludes, as taking place *under the gospel-dispensation?* Yet *this world,* if we may credit Wahl, was now no more, inasmuch as the *world to come* had already begun.

Let any one now examine Mark 4: 19. Luke 20: 34. Rom. 12: 2. 1 Cor. 1: 20. 2: 6. 2: 8. 2 Cor. 4: 4. Gal. 1: 4. 2 Tim. 4: 10. Tit. 2: 12. Matt. 13: 40, 49. 28: 20, and see what these texts can possibly have to do exclusively with the age that *preceded* the Messiah. And yet, if Wahl be in the right, they all fall under this class, having a relation more or less distinct to such an age.

How easy to be misled, when we fall upon *theory* that looks attractive! Wahl fell upon the above theory, in Bertholdt's *Christologia Judaeorum* etc. p. 38 seq., and thought it would solve many apparent difficulties about *αἰών* in the New Testrment. But the theory itself, like many other things in that undigested and hasty book, needs much more confirmation than has been given to it, before it can be so extensively applied as Wahl has applied it.

The remarks which I have just made, on the meaning assigned by Wahl to *present* and *future αἰών,* will apply, in all respects, to the article on this same word in the Lexicon of Bretschneider; who, under the same guide (Bertholdt), has fallen into the same errors.

Had he and Wahl simply read, with attention, the article עוֹלָם in Buxtorf's immortal Hebrew, Rabbinic, and Chaldaic Lexicon, they might have avoided such a mistake. This Coryphaeus of all Rabbinical investiga-

§ 19. *Does αἰώνιος mean spiritual?*

tors, has given no occasion that any attentive and intelligent reader should be misled.

But it is time to retreat from the examination of Lexicons. Enough has been said, I trust, to put the student on his guard against implicitly following the authority of dictionaries; especially in respect to an important article like the present, and when the *whole* of the evidence is not laid before him.

I must beg leave, in closing, to make a few remarks on a singular criticism upon the word αἰώνιος, which I have recently met with in one of the Journals of the day.

The writer proposes to render αἰώνιος, *spiritual*. His reason is, that Aeons (*Αἰῶνες*) were counted as incorporeal, i. e. spiritual, beings; and therefore αἰώνιος, may mean *Aeonic*, i. e. *spiritual*. In accordance with this, he construes the various passages which exhibit αἰώνιος, and which have a relation to future punishment.

This criticism has, at least, the merit of novelty. At all events it is novel to me, inasmuch as I never met with it in any writer before; nor did it once ever occur to my mind, as a probable or possible meaning of αἰώνιος. But then, the author of it might very justly say; 'This is no good argument against the probability of the criticism; much less against the *possibility* of it; and a better ground than this may very properly be demanded, for rejecting it.'

I cannot deny the reasonableness of this; and I therefore, out of respect to one who appears to be seriously inquiring after Scriptural truth, would suggest the following grounds, why I must reject the exegesis which he has proffered.

1. The question remains to be settled, whether the

§ 19. *Does αἰώνιος mean spiritual?* 73

Gnostic system, (the one from which the imagination of *Aeons* sprung), had an existence, or at any rate, was known in the western parts of Asia, before the propagation of the gospel, or even at that period. Whoever has read Tittmann, *de Vestigiis Gnosticorum in Nov. Test. frustra quaesitis*, will have vehement doubts, as I must think, in regard to the point in question ; more vehement still, whether the New Testament exhibits any certain marks, that the writers of it had an acquaintance with the *Aeonic* system.

The Aeons were, (if we may credit the statement of the Gnostics who believed in their existence), beings of both good and bad characters, i. e. there were some of each, belonging to the different classes. They were regarded as *secondary* or *derived divinities*, θεοὶ δεύτεροι. There were spiritual beings above them, and below them. Why then should *Aeonic*, be chosen to designate *spiritual*, any more than an adjective borrowed from the name of the God above them, or the sub-divinities below them ?

But how dubious, too, must such an adjective be! The majority of the Aeons were *apostate* ones. *Aeonic*, then, would be about the same as *diabolic*, in regard to its meaning. Suppose now, I should assert, that *diabolic* means *spiritual*, because the devil is a *spiritual* being; would this be a well-chosen epithet to supply the place of *spiritual?* Can it be probable, then, that *Aeonic punishment* and *Aeonic life*, are used by the New Testament writers to denote *spiritual* punishment and *spiritual* happiness? If it could be shewn, (which it cannot be), that the New Testament writers had an acquaintance with the system of the Gnostics ; it must still appear very improbable that they would coin such an unfortunate adjective as *Aeonic*. But until we are better ascertained

§ 19. *Does αἰώνιος mean spiritual?*

whether they knew any thing about Aeons, we can never be entitled to give such an exegesis to their writings.

2. But there is another conclusive argument against the interpretation in question. This is, that the exegesis proposed would make *spiritual misery* or *happiness* to begin only *after* the general judgement. Matt. 25: 31 —46 represents, (as the critic in question concedes), the judgement of the *future world.* Is it then true, that *spiritual* happiness commences with the righteous only after that period ; or that *spiritual* misery then first begins with the wicked? Neither the one nor the other; and consequently I cannot admit the exegesis, which, without any support at all from philology, would force me to such a conclusion.

3. But if the meaning *spiritual,* is to be given to αἰώνιος, as a general one in the New Testament, then cases would arise of the most revolting nature, in regard to the application of it. For example ; 1 Tim. 6: 16, [to God] be κράτος αἰώνιον. Shall we render, *spiritual power ?*

Heb. 9: 14, who [Christ] by an *eternal Spirit,* διὰ πνεύματος αἰωνίου, offered up himself, etc. Shall we say, *by a spiritual Spirit ?*

Philemon, v. 15, for he (Onesimus) was absent a little while, that thou mightest have him αἰώνιον—*spiritually ?*

Rom. 16: 25, the revelation of the mystery, which was kept in silence χρόνοις αἰωνίοις·—*in the spiritual ages ?*

2 Tim. 1: 9, the grace given us . . . . πρὸ χρόνων αἰωνίων·—*before the spiritual ages ?*

But I have pursued this illustration far enough. I know not how to think that the writer on whom I am an-

§ 19. *Does αἰώνιος mean spiritual?*

imadverting, can seriously persuade himself that he has made out a philological argument in favour of his position. If not, then why should he venture to urge such a position on his readers? when in his own conscience he must know, that grounds of reasoning *a priori* have inclined him to embrace the doctrine which rejects the *eternity* of future punishment; and not the language of the Bible. Let him shew that a day of grace, a preached gospel, an offered Mediator, a sanctifying Spirit, and pardoning mercy, are proclaimed in the Scriptures as proffered to sinners in another world, who have rejected them all in this; and then we may lend him a listening ear. Until then, we must believe that "the unjust will be unjust still; and the filthy, filthy still."

שׁאוֹל

§ 1. *Usual meaning of the word.*

The word שׁאוֹל has, not unfrequently, been derived by lexicographers and critics, from the root שָׁאַל, *to ask, crave, demand, require, seek for*, etc. Now inasmuch as the *grave* may be figuratively said to be *rapacious* or *craving*, it has been supposed that the name in question was therefore given to the *grave* or *under-world;* and that שׁאוֹל means, in Hebrew, what *Orcus rapax* does in Latin, or the same as *insatiable sepulchre* does in English.

This etymology, however, is too uncertain, to be entitled to much confidence. Nor is the origin of the word in question, in any good degree illustrated by any of the languages kindred with the Hebrew. Of these, the Syriac and Ethiopic only exhibit the word; but not in such a manner as to cast any important light on its etymology. We are left, therefore, merely to the manner in which the Hebrews employed the word, in order to determine its meaning. The examples of it, in the Hebrew Scriptures are somewhat numerous; still as an investigation of its real import must be a matter of deep interest to every serious inquirer, it seems necessary to bring the whole of them into view.

§ 1. *Meaning of* שְׁאוֹל. 77

I observe, by way of introduction to the view of them which is now to be given, that I have simply followed, as my custom is, the *Concordance*, and endeavoured, in each case, to determine the meaning of the word שְׁאוֹל, from the connexion in which it stands.

The arrangement with regard to the respective meanings of the word in question, which I have thought to be the most plain and lucid, is as follows ; viz.

I. THE MORE OBVIOUS OR LITERAL SENSE OF SHEÔL.

This is, *the under-world, the region of the dead, the grave, the sepulchre, the region of ghosts* or *departed spirits.*

This meaning is *general*, i. e. the signification of the word שְׁאוֹל is *generic*. In other words, it sometimes signifies the *region of the dead*, to which the righteous and the wicked both go ; as does ᾅδης, *the invisible world*, in classic Greek authors. But as every *generic* word is capable also of a *specific* meaning, whan circumstances require it; so, we shall see in the sequel, *Sheôl* may be regarded sometimes as the place to which good men go after their death, and sometimes as the place to which evil men go ; i. e. the word itself means, *the region of the dead in general*, and it is made *particular*, only by circumstances connected with it.

I proceed to detail the examples.

Gen. 37: 35, and [Jacob] said, I will go down *into the grave*, שְׁאֹלָה, unto my son, mourning ; i. e. Jacob declares that he shall be brought down to the grave by mourning, and thus be united wih Joseph his son, whom he believed to have been destroyed by wild beasts. It is not to be supposed, that Jacob believed Joseph to have gone to *the world of wo*, *to hell* in the common sense of

8

§ 1. *Meaning of* שְׁאוֹל.

this word as it is now used by us; nor that he himself expected to go thither. Indeed, it is impossible to mistake the obvious meaning of *Sheól* here, which is simply *grave* or *region of the dead*.

Gen. 42: 38, [Jacob says], ye shall bring down my gray hairs with sorrow to *Sheól*, שְׁאוֹלָה; i. e. simply to the grave, as before.

Gen. 44: 29, [Jacob says], ye shall bring down my gray hairs with sorrow to the grave, שְׁאֹלָה; the same as above.

Gen. 44: 31, [Judah says to Joseph, when pleading for the liberation of his brother Benjamin], We shall bring down the gray hairs of thy servant, our father, with sorrow to the grave, שְׁאוֹלָה; in the same sense as above.

Num. 16: 30, [Moses says of Korah and his company], If .... the earth open her mouth, and swallow them up .... and they go down alive into *Sheól*, שְׁאֹלָה; i. e. if they go down alive into the under-world, into the region of the dead. That Korah and his company went to the world of wo, there can indeed be but little if any reason to doubt, considering their character and the nature of their crime. But the words of Moses in this place, seem to refer *primarily* to the event which was about to take place, viz. to Korah and his adherents being swallowed up alive, and thus going down into the under-world.

Num. 16: 33, they [i. e. Korah and his company] went down alive into *Sheól*, שְׁאֹלָה; i. e. they went down alive into the under-world, the region of the dead.

In the two last cited passages, our English version has *pit*, as the translation of *Sheól*. The sense of *pit* is *grave, deep cavity* or *recess in the earth*. The sense of *hell*, given to the word *pit* by occasional usage, is figurative or secondary, and not the literal or primary meaning of it.

§ 4. *Meaning of* שְׁאוֹל.

Deut. 32: 22, for a fire is kindled in mine anger, and it shall burn to the lowest *Sheól*, שְׁאוֹל תַּחְתִּית; i. e. it shall burn down into the very under-world. So the parallelism in the sequel leads us to interpret this; which runs thus, "It shall set on fire the foundations of the mountains." The image is a tremendous one, viz. that of a fire so intense and dreadful, as not only to consume all that is on the surface of the ground, but to burn deep down into *the under-world*.

1 Sam. 2: 6. The Lord killeth, and maketh alive; he bringeth down to *Sheól*, שְׁאוֹל, and bringeth up; i. e. he bringeth down to the grave or region of the dead, and bringeth or raiseth up from the same. That such is the meaning of this passage, seems plain from the first part of the verse, in which it is said, The Lord killeth and maketh alive; the equivalent of which is, The Lord bringeth down to *Sheól*, and raiseth up from it. If by *Sheól* here, *hell*, (in its appropriate sense), be meant; then how shall the last clause be construed, viz. The Lord *bringeth up from Sheól?* Is it then a Scripture doctrine, that the Lord brings up from the "eternal pit," those who are once confined there? Or rather, do not the Scriptures teach that "the smoke of their torment ascendeth up forever and ever?"

2 Sam. 22: 6, the snares of *Sheól*, שְׁאוֹל, encompassed me; the deadly nets came upon me. Our English version renders thus; "The sorrows of hell compassed me about; the snares of death prevented me," i. e. *came before* me; for this is the sense in which the word *prevent* is employed, in our version, and not in the sense of *hinder*, which would here misrepresent the Hebrew. This version evidently sacrifices the parallelism of the original Hebrew; in which חֶבְלֵי שְׁאוֹל, *the snares of*

§ 1. *Meaning of* שְׁאוֹל.

Sheól, and מוֹקְשֵׁי מָוֶת, *the nets* or *snares of death*, are equivalents. It seems to sacrifice propriety also; for in what tolerable sense could David say, that *the sorrows of hell* (in our present sense of this word) encompased him? But when, in describing a scene of the highest danger, he is represented as saying, figuratively, 'The snares *of Sheól* encompassed me, i. e. such fatal snares as take hold of their victim with deadly force, or subject him to death; such snares as bring their victim down to the region of the dead; then all is plain and proper. Then too, the parallelism with the second part of the same verse is retained; which is, " The snares of death came upon me." On the whole, the case is so plain, that no rational doubt can be entertained, by any one versed in the original languages of the Bible, with regard to its real meaning. Comp. Ps. 18: 5 (6).

1 K. 2: 6, [David, charging Solomon to punish Joab for the murders he had committed, says], Thou shalt not let his hoary head go down to *Sheól*, שְׁאֹל, in peace; i. e. thou shalt not let him die a natural death, but shalt punish him, or put him to a violent death. So our translators; who have here translated שְׁאֹל by the word *grave*, thus shewing how they understood the passage.

1 K. 2: 9, [David, charging Solomon to punish Shimei, says], Thou shalt bring down his hoary head to *Sheól* with blood; i. e. thou shalt cause him to suffer a violent death, and not leave him to die a natural one. The passage is of the same nature as that above; and שְׁאוֹל is also rendered *grave* here, by our English translators. The meaning of *Sheól*, in both cases, may be expressed by *grave*, or *region of the dead, under-world*.

Job 7: 9, As a cloud is consumed and vanisheth away; so he that goeth down to *Sheól*, shall come up no

§ 1. *Meaning of* שְׁאוֹל.

more ; i. e. he that goeth down to the grave, to the region of the dead, shall no more return to the present world— never rise up again to mix with the living here. So our translators understood the word *Sheól* here, inasmuch as they have rendered it, *grave*.

Job 11: 8, It is as high as heaven, what canst thou do ? Deeper than *Sheól*, מִשְּׁאוֹל , what canst thou know ? i. e. deeper than the under-world, the abyss, the world beneath ; for the antithesis of heaven, i. e. the natural heaven, lofty, elevated beyond admeasurement, is plainly intended here ; and this antithesis can be none other than the abyss beneath, the under-world, Hades. Our version, which here renders *hell*, has obscured the exact meaning of the passage.

Job 14: 13, O that thou would hide me in *Sheól*, בִּשְׁאוֹל ; i. e. in the grave, or (in other words) O that I might die!

This is one of those cases, about which there can be no possible doubt. Job might, as thousands of others have done, wish for death, in a time when deep distress and despondency had come upon him ; but surely Job did not wish to be placed in the world of wo, in hell. Accordingly, our translators have here rendered *Sheól* by *grave*.

Job 17: 13, If I wait, *Sheól* is my house ; i. e. let me die speedily, for if I should continue ever so long in life, I must die at last, or go down to the grave. So our translators , " The *grave* is mine house."

Job 17: 16, They shall go down to the bars of *Sheol*, when our rest together is in the dust ; i. e. they shall go down into the grave, together shall we rest in the dust, viz. in the grave or sepulchre. Here our translation has *pit ;* which (if it mean *grave* as I suppose it does) is correct as to the idea conveyed by the passage. The place of future punishment cannot be meant here; for surely Job did not expect to go to such a place; nor were corruption and the worm, (which, as he here avers, were to 'rest together with him in the dust'), to go with him to a place of future punishment.

Job 24: 19, drought and heat consume the snow waters; so doth *the grave*, שְׁאוֹל, those who have sinned. So our Version; and rightly, for the consumption of the body in the grave, is clearly the idea here, which the writer designs to express.

Job 26: 6, *Sheól*, שְׁאוֹל, is naked before him, and destruction, אֲבַדּוֹן, hath no covering; i. e. the under-world, the world beneath, is open to his all-seeing eye, yea, the place of destruction, viz. the grave, hath no covering. The idea here is plainly of this nature; for the object of the writer is, to place in a striking point of view, the omniscience of God. In order to do this, he represents him as extending his view to the dark world beneath, as well as to all parts of the earth that lie exposed to the light of day. But our translators have here rendered *Sheól* by the word *hell;* for which I am not able to see any good reason.

Ps. 6: 5 (6), For in death there is no remembrance of thee; in *Sheol*, בִּשְׁאוֹל, who shall give thee thanks? i. e. in the world of the dead, who shall present thank offerings for deliverance from danger? How can offerings of this nature be made, when fatal evils have overtaken me? The first member of the verse, 'In death there is no remembrance of thee,' shews the meaning of the second member; and of course the meaning of *Sheol*, which may be rendered, *sepulchre, under-world*, or, as our Version has it, *grave*.

It will be remembered, that the Psalmist is here

§ 1. *Meaning of* שְׁאוֹל.

speaking of his own danger, and praying for deliverance. Can it be well supposed that he means to express the idea, that if cut off he should go to the world of woe, to *hell*, where no praise could be given to God?

Ps. 16: 10, 'Thou wilt not leave my soul [me] in *Sheol*, לִשְׁאוֹל; neither wilt thou suffer thy Holy One to see corruption; i. e. thou wilt not leave me in the grave, nor suffer thy consecrated Messiah to consume, or to be turned to corruption there. In other words, thou wilt raise me from the dead, before the grave exercises the power of corruption over me. So Peter construes this passage, in Acts 2: 24—32, applying it simply to the resurrection of Christ from the grave. Indeed, no evidence is needed besides the nature of the parallelism in the verse, inasmuch as the latter member explains the former. We might ask, also, can the soul of Jesus be supposed to have been in the *world of woe, the place of the damned?* I know, indeed, that there are some, who deduce from this passage the doctrine of a *purgatory*, into which Christ descended, in order to preach to " the spirits who are in prison." But there is no foundation in this text, for any such deduction.

Ps. 18: 5 (6), The cords of *Sheol*, שְׁאוֹל, encompassed me; the snares of death came upon me; i. e. the deadly cords encompassed me. See on 2 Sam. 22: 6 above. The English Version here (*hell*) has plainly failed to give the appropriate meaning; i. e. this is so, provided the word *hell* be understood as meaning *the world of woe*.

Ps. 30: 3 (4), Thou hast brought up my soul from *Sheol*, מִן שְׁאוֹל; i. e. thou hast kept me alive, amidst great dangers, so that I did not go down to the pit. Here our version has *grave;* for, indeed, any other version

§ 1. *Meaning of* שְׁאוֹל.

would have been an evident departure from the meaning of the writer; who surely does not mean to say, in this place, that he had been brought up *from the world of woe.* He is celebrating the goodness of God in " preserving him alive, and keeping him from going down to the pit."

Ps. 31: 17 (18), let the wicked be ashamed, and let them be silent in *Sheol,* לִשְׁאוֹל; i. e. let them be cut off, or let them be punished with the loss of life. If we construe *Sheol* here as meaning *the world of future misery,* it would represent the Psalmist as praying that the wicked might be sent to that world; an example of which can hardly be found, I believe, in the Scriptures; nor is it easy for a benevolent mind well to conceive, how a good man could pray directly for such an object as this. On the other hand, if Sheol be rendered *grave* here, as it is in our English Version, then we may conceive it altogether possible, that a good man, a magistrate and a king, whose duty it was to cut off certain transgressors, might express a wish that the justice due to them in a *civil* respect, might be executed.

Ps. 49: 14 (15), Like sheep they [the wicked] are laid in *Sheol,* לִשְׁאוֹל . . . . their beauty shall consume in *Sheol,* or be for the consuming of *Sheol,* לְבַלּוֹת שְׁאוֹל. Here, that they are laid in *Sheol* like sheep, is a circumstance which points to the *grave,* and not primarily to *the world of woe;* and so the last part of the verse also indicates, by *the consuming of Sheol,* viz. the consumption or corruption of the flesh in the grave. So, also, our English translators understood the passage, having rendered *Sheol* by the word *grave,* in both cases.

Ps. 49: 15 (16), But God will redeem my soul [me] from the power of *Sheol,* מִיַּד שְׁאוֹל, i. e. from *Sheol.* In

§ 1. *Meaning of* שְׁאוֹל.

other words, God will preserve me from the grave; he will keep me from perishing like the wicked. Whether, under this imagery, more than a *literal* meaning is not here conveyed, as also in the example above, will be a matter of inquiry in the sequel.

Ps. 55: 15 (16), Let death seize upon them; let them go down alive into Sheol, יֵרְדוּ שְׁאוֹל חַיִּים; i. e. let the grave or the under-world swallow them up alive. In other words, Let them be speedily and in a fearful manner punished, or cut off. In respect to the sentiment, I would refer the reader to what is said on Ps. 31: 17 above. There is a serious difficulty in the way of supposing the Psalmist to have prayed, that his enemies should go down suddenly to the world of future woe. Here, however, our English Version renders *Sheol* by *hell;* but why this should be done here, and not in Ps. 31: 17, it would be difficult to say.

Ps. 86: 13, great is thy mercy toward me; and thou hast delivered my soul [me] from the lowest *Sheol*, מִשְׁאוֹל תַּחְתִּיָּה. At first view, it would seem as if the Psalmist were here speaking of spiritual deliverance from hell, or the world of future misery, and thanking God, that by his mercy he had provided a way of escape from it. But the next verse seems plainly to indicate, that deliverance from temporal death is here meant. It runs thus; " O God! the proud are risen up against me; and the assemblies of violent men have sought after my soul [my life], and have not set thee before them." The word נֶפֶשׁ, which our translators have here rendered *soul*, is a common Hebrew word for *life*, and is very often so rendered. It clearly has that meaning here; for *soul*, in any other sense than this, David's enemies surely did not seek after. Consequently, we must conclude, that the

§ 1. *Meaning of* שְׁאוֹל.

deliverance commemorated in v. 13, is a deliverance from the grave, or under-world, i. e. from death. By saying *lowest grave* or *sepulchre*, the writer designates a most terrible and cruel death, or a death of the most shocking nature.

Ps. 88: 4, My soul is full of trouble; my life draweth near to *Sheol*, לִשְׁאוֹל; i. e. to the grave, as our English Version has expressed it. The context clearly shews this; in which the writer goes on to say, that he is "like the slain that lie in the grave;" and asks whether God will "shew wonders to the dead, etc." He says also, "Thou hast laid me in the lowest pit;" which will illustrate *lowest Sheol* in Ps. 86: 13.

Ps. 89: 48 (49), What man is he that liveth and shall not see death? Shall he deliver his soul [life] from the hand of *Sheol?* שְׁאוֹל; i. e. from the power of the grave. So our Version, "from the hand of the grave." The first clause of the verse makes the sense of *grave*, in the latter clause, to be certain.

Ps. 116: 3, The sorrows of death encompassed me; the pains of *Sheol*, שְׁאוֹל, took hold upon me; i. e. deadly pains, such as lead to death, or occasion death, took hold upon me. See on Sam. 22: 6, and Ps. 18: 5 above.

Ps. 139: 8, If I ascend to heaven thou art there; if I make my bed in *Sheol* שְׁאוֹל, thou art there; i. e. if I ascend upwards, on high, thou art there; or if I go downwards, into the world beneath, thou art there; which is as much as to say, Thou art everywhere, or in all places. More than this cannot with any certainty be deduced from this passage; indeed, more than this is altogether improbable.

Ps. 141: 7, Our bones are scattered at the mouth of *Sheol;* i. e. at the mouth of the sepulchre or grave, as our

Version has it; not at the mouth of *hell* or the *world of woe.*

Prov. 1: 12. Let us swallow them up alive, as *the grave*, כִּשְׁאוֹל; and whole, as those who go down to the pit. So our English Version; and plainly, according to the sense of the Original. The writer is repeating the words of men of violence and blood, who are mutually exhorting one another to the work of destruction. The meaning of their words is, Let us kill or destroy, as *Sheol* does, i. e. extensively and fatally as the grave.

Prov. 15: 11, *Sheol and destruction*, שְׁאוֹל וַאֲבַדּוֹן, are before the Lord; how much more the hearts of the children of men? English Version, *hell*. But here the under-world, the deep, dark, secret world, seems plainly to be meant. So the accompanying word, אֲבַדּוֹן, seems clearly to imply. The sentiment is; 'God, whose sight penetrates even the dark recesses of the grave or under-world, most certainly must know what passes in the hearts of the children of men.'

Prov. 27: 20, *Sheol*, שְׁאוֹל, and destruction are never satiated; so the eyes of a man are never satisfied; i. e. the grave and the place of destruction, viz. the sepulchre or under-world, are insatiable; in other words, death is always making its ravages, and is never satiated. So the Latins, *mors rapax, orcus rapax.* The nature of the imagery here, requires us to understand *Sheol* as meaning *grave;* and not, with our English translation, *hell.*

Prov. 30: 15, 16, There are three things which are never satisfied, yea four things say not, It is enough; the grave (שְׁאוֹל), the barren womb, the earth that is not filled with water, and the fire that saith not, It is enough. Here *Sheol* is correctly rendered in our common version. But the same reason which led to render it *grave* here,

§ 1. *Meaning of* שְׁאוֹל.

applies in its full force to Prov. 27: 20, where is the same image and the same sentiment.

Ecc. 9: 10, there is no work, nor device, nor knowledge, nor wisdom, in *Sheol*, בִּשְׁאוֹל, whither thou goest; i. e. as our English Version has it, in *the grave*, whither thou goest. This is plainly the sense of the passage; 'Be very diligent while life continues; for death will quickly intervene, and then all purposes and efforts, such as you are engaged in, will cease.'

Cant. 8: 6, love is strong as death; jealousy is cruel as *Sheol;* English Version, cruel as the *grave*. This is plainly the sense; for the imagery is here taken, from the unsparing, cruel, and irresistible power of the grave or death; which jealousy resembles, when it is highly excited.

Is. 5: 14, Therefore *Sheol*, שְׁאוֹל, hath enlarged herself, and opened her mouth without measure; English Version, *hell*. But here, the *under-world* or *region of the dead* is personified, and represented as a great, terrible, and insatiable monster, opening wide its jaws, even without measure, in order to swallow up and devour the intemperate revellers, who are mentioned in the preceding context. It is an image of the like nature with that which is presented in Prov. 27: 20. 30: 16.

[Note. Is. 7: 11 is inserted in Calasio's Concordance, as an instance of *Sheol*. But the word here, according to the best copies of the Hebrew Bible, is שְׁאֵלָה, *request, petition;* not שְׁאֹלָה, *Sheol*.]

Is. 14: 9, *Sheol*, שְׁאוֹל, from beneath is moved for thee, to meet thee at thy coming. The prophet is speaking of the king of Babylon, who was to be slain, and when he should go down into the *under-world* or *Sheol*, the ghosts or *umbrae* of the dead there would rise up to meet

§ 1. *Meaning of* שְׁאוֹל.

him with insult and contumely. Our English Version renders *Sheol, hell*. But plainly *the region of the dead, the land of ghosts* is here meant; for in verse 18, 'all the kings of the nations are said to repose *in glory there,* i. e. to lie in their sepulchres, attended with all the ensigns of splendor which were deposited around the bodies of deceased kings.

Is. 14: 15, yet thou [the king of Babylon] shalt be brought down to *Sheol*, שְׁאוֹל; English Version, *hell*. The word here is most evidently in the same sense as above; for so the parallelism which follows clearly shews, viz. " to the sides of the pit."

Is. 28: 15, ye have said, We have a covenant with *death*, and with *Sheol*, שְׁאוֹל, are we at agreement; English Version, *hell*. The meaning is, ' We have covenanted with *death* and *Sheol,* i. e. the *grave,* not to seize upon us, not to harm us. So the sequel shews; for the prophet represents them as next saying, "When the overflowing scourge shall pass through, it shall not come unto us."

Is. 28: 18, your covenant with death shall be disannulled; your agreement with *Sheol,* שְׁאוֹל, shall not stand; English Version, *hell*. This is a repetition of the passage above, in which the words, of course, are employed in the same sense.

Is. 38: 18, For *Sheol,* שְׁאוֹל, cannot praise thee; death cannot celebrate thee; English Version of *Sheol, grave*. The meaning here is plain, viz. How can the dead, or those in the sepulchre praise thee ? Surely we cannot well suppose Hezekiah means to say here, that *hell*, i. e. the world of torment, cannot praise God. He did not expect to perish forever, when he should die.

But when he says, " *Sheol* cannot praise thee," does

§ 1. *Meaning of* שְׁאוֹל.

he mean, that after death there is no ability to praise God, no existence of the powers and capacities of the soul? I think not. It seems to me clearly, that this is not his design; although not a few of the later critics have affirmed it to be so. Shall we represent the Hebrews, and a Hebrew monarch enlightened as Hezekiah was, as being more ignorant in respect to futurity than the Egyptians? The people of God, who lived under the light of a revelation, more ignorant than those who were in the midst of Egyptian night! Believe this who will, I must have stronger evidence of its correctness than I have yet found, in order to give it credit.

I regard the simple meaning of this controverted place, (and of others like it, e. g. Ps. 6: 5 (6). 30: 9 (10). 88: 11. 115: 17. comp. 118: 17), as being this, viz. 'The dead can no more give thanks to God, nor celebrate his praises, among the living on earth, and thus cause his name to be glorified by them, or thus do him honour before them. So the sequel of Is. 38: 18; "The living, the living, he shall praise thee; as I do this day: the father to the children shall make known thy truth, i. e. thy faithfulness." This last clause makes the whole plain; and one is ready to wonder, that so much skepticism about the views of the Hebrews in regard to a future state of existence, could have been eked out of the verse in question.

Is. 57: 9, and [thou] didst debase thyself even to *Sheol*, שְׁאוֹל. The prophet is addressing the idolatrous Jews here, who are represented under the image of an unchaste female, debasing herself by her vile practices. There is a kind of paronomasia here upon the word *Sheol.* "Thou didst debase thyself to Sheol," means thou didst prostrate thyself *very low;* and the force of the word

§ 1. *Meaning of* שְׁאוֹל.

consists in referring both to the physical and moral debasement of a prostitute. The sense of *Sheol*, which is referred to or built upon in the figurative use of it here, is *under-world, the world deep beneath.*

Ezek. 31: 15, in the day when he went down to *Sheol*, שְׁאֹלָה, I caused a mourning; English Version, *grave.* Rightly, for the prophet is speaking of the death of the king of Egypt.

Ezek. 31: 16, when I cast him down to *Sheol*, שְׁאֹלָה, with them that descend into the pit; English Version, *hell.* But as the subject is the same, and the affirmation clearly the same, as in the preceding verse; so the version should be, *grave.*

Ezek. 31: 17, They also went down into *Sheol* (שְׁאֹלָה) with him, unto them that be slain with the sword; English Version, *hell.* But plainly, the whole relates to *physical* death here, not to spiritual. So the context clearly shews.

Ezek. 32: 21, The strong among the mighty [the mighty heroes], shall address him from *Sheol*, שְׁאוֹל; English Version, *hell.* Here, the king of Egypt is spoken of, and described as falling by the sword with other men of war, and going down to *Sheol*, where he is addressed, (as the king of Babylon is represented to be in Is. 14: 9 seq.), by the רְפָאִים, *the umbrae* in the under-world. Of course, *grave, region of the dead*, must be the meaning of *Sheol* here.

Ezek. 32: 27, They shall not lie with the mighty that are fallen of the uncircumcised; which are gone down to *Sheol* (שְׁאוֹל) with their weapons of war; English Version, *hell.* But are "the weapons of war," then, carried along with fallen heroes to *the world of future punishment?* Or are they merely buried with them, according to a very common usage, in the *grave?*

§ 1. *Meaning of* שְׁאוֹל.

Hos. 13: 14, I will ransom them from Sheol; O death, I will be thy plagues! O *Sheol*, שְׁאוֹל, I will be thy destruction! English Version, *grave*. If this be not the sense, then the sacred writer has declared, that God will be the *destruction* of the *world of woe;* i. e. that he will destroy it, or bring it to an end; a sentiment for which I can find no parallel in the Scriptures. But God has often declared, that the power of the *grave* shall cease, i. e. that a resurrection from the dead or the grave shall take place. This is, of course, to *destroy Sheol*, i. e. to disannul its power.

Amos 9: 2, Though they dig into *Sheol*, שְׁאוֹל, my hand shall take them thence; English Version, *hell*. The sense clearly is, 'Although they dig *very deep*, down *into the under-world*, viz. in order to conceal themselves, yet thence my hand shall take them [the wicked.]

Jonah 2: 2 (3), out of the belly of *Sheol* I cried; and thou didst hear my voice; English Version, *hell*. But Jonah was not in *hell*, i. e. not in the place of future torment, but in the belly of the fish, and *deep down*, under the surface of the water. So the meaning of *under-world* here, is very obvious.

Hab. 2: 5, Who [the Chaldean] enlargeth his appetite as *Sheol*, כִּשְׁאוֹל, and like death cannot be satisfied, English Version, *hell*. But here the sense is plainly the same as above, in Prov. 27: 20. 30: 16. Is. 5: 14; i. e. the passage refers to the insatiable appetite of death (mors rapax), or the grave.

These are all the passages in which the word *Sheol*, שְׁאוֹל, appears to me to occur, in the Old Testament, in the sense given under No. I, above. On these, thus presented in detail before the reader, I must beg leave now to make a few remarks.

§ 2. *Remarks on the common translation of Sheol.*

There can be no reasonable doubt, that *Sheol* does most generally mean *the under-world, the grave* or *sepulchre, the world of the dead*, in the Old Testament Scriptures. It is very clear that there are many passages, where no other meaning can reasonably be assigned to it. Accordingly, our English translators have rendered the word Sheol *grave*, in 30 instances* out of the whole 64 instances in which it occurs in the Hebrew Scriptures. In many of the remaining cases, where they have given a different version of the word, i. e. translated it *hell*, it is equally clear that it should have been rendered, *grave* or *region of the dead*. This has been clearly shewn, by producing the instances in the above exhibition of examples.

In *three* cases, they have recognized the same principle, (at least this seems to have been their view), viz. Numb. 16: 30, 33. Job 17: 16, where it is translated, *pit*.

In regard to most of the cases in which they have rendered the word *hell*, it may be doubtful whether they meant thereby to designate *the world of future torment*. The incongruity of such a rendering, at least in not a few cases, has been already pointed out, in the citations of the respective examples above, and therefore need not be here repeated. The inconstancy with which they have sometimes rendered the word *Sheol*, in the same

---

* The instances are in Gen. 37: 35. 42: 38. 44: 29, 31. 1 Sam. 2: 6. 1 Kings 2: 6, 9. Job 7: 9. 14: 13. 17: 13. 21: 13. 24: 19. Ps. 6: 5. 30: 3. 31: 17. 49: 14, 15. 88: 3. 89: 49. 141: 7. Prov. 1: 12. 30: 16. Ecc. 9: 10. Cant. 8: 6. Is. 14: 11. 38: 10, 18. Ezek. 31: 15. Hos. 13: 14 bis.

§ 2. Remarks on the translation of *Sheol.*

connection and with the same sense, is a striking circumstance, which cannot but be regarded with some wonder by an attentive inquirer. Nor is this always to be attributed to *different* translators, (who are known to have been employed in making the English version); but the *same* translator has been occasionally inconsistent with himself; e. g. Ezek. 31: 15, compared with Ezek. 31: 16, 17.

But setting aside all this, and simply recurring to the Original as a foundation for our exegesis, is there not some reason to believe, that in some of the cases where *Sheol* is employed, it stands as a word employed in a secondary sense, in order to designate *the future world of woe?*

An interesting question; the solution of which depends on the nature of figurative language, and the manner in which it is employed, in order to designate the things of a future world.

§ 3. *Manner of using figurative language, in respect to the objects of a future world.*

On the nature of figurative language, then, as employed to designate the objects of the invisible world, I must beg leave here to suggest a few considerations, which may serve more fully to explain what I shall say in the sequel.

Spoken language is the expression of ideas by means of sounds, i. e. articulate words. Written language is the expression of ideas by means of conventional signs, i. e. letters, which are presented to the eye, and through the medium of this, find access to the mind. Both spoken and written language is merely the expression of our

§ 3. *Nature of figurative language.*

ideas. Both agree in this, viz. that they are *conventional;* conventional I mean, as to the particular sounds or forms of which they consist. That language is natural to man, as much so as understanding and reason are, is what I fully believe. But that there may be a great variety of sounds employed, in order to convey the same idea; that, for example, different individuals may call *the Sun* by names of very different sounds, all know to be matter of fact. But this would not prove that the faculty of speech is not a constituent part of the nature of man. It only proves, that there are various ways in which this faculty may be exercised.

I call spoken language, therefore, conventional as to its *form* or *sounds*, merely because nature does not make any *one* language universal and necessary; and what is not universal and necessary, may with propriety be called *conventional*, using this word in a modified sense of it, to denote what results from the voluntary agreement and usages of men.

In the same manner all written language is *conventional*. Every nation has its own peculiar modes of writing; some of which differ very widely from others, not only in the forms of letters, but in the letters or alphabets themselves.

But all language, whether spoken or written, being only the expression of ideas which are entertained by the human mind; an important question remains respecting these ideas themselves, viz. What are the sources of them? Or, whence does the mind derive them? When this question is answered, others can easily be raised, which stand in close connection with it.

It is now pretty generally agreed, (at least in the English world, so far as I know), that the sources of all

§ 3. *Nature of figurative language.*

our definite ideas, are *sensation, reflection,* and *consciousness.* [May we not add, *moral nature ?*] Some might contend against *consciousness,* because they resolve it into reminiscence of experience either by sensation or reflection. This however is not important to my purpose. The fact is all I wish for here ; not to settle the question by what name it shall be called.

But how extensive are the objects of our senses, and of reflection and consciousness ? Plainly they are limited to the visible, perceptible, external world without us, and to our own internal man. All language is formed merely to designate, in its *original* use, the ideas which we derive from the one or the other of these sources. If we go beyond this circle, and strive to express conceptions of other objects, the mind employs the words which already exist, and which have originated from one of the sources above mentioned, in a secondary, a qualified, or a figurative sense. It traces some analogy between things within the circle of its knowledge, with those which are believed to lie beyond the boundaries of its immediate perception, and applies language in such a manner as accords with this supposed analogy.

For example, and that I may more fully illustrate my meaning ; God is not the object of any of our senses, internal or external. But by the powers of reason, and by the force of the moral nature that exists within us, we arrive at a conviction, that there must exist, and that there does exist, a Being above us, of almighty power, and of infinite wisdom, who has created, and who governs all things. We undertake to describe him. But we have not seen him ; we have not, in any way, been able to subject him, as he is in himself, to the examination of any of our faculties. The language that we speak did not

§ 3. *Nature of figurative language.*

originate from those who had ever formed any conceptions of the Divinity through the medium of their senses. Of course, we have no words which directly convey to us, by themselves, the idea of God as he is in himself. We can only describe him, by language employed in the way of analogy. We regard him as a rational being; and as such, we borrow terms, descriptive in themselves of the various parts or passions and affections of men, in order to convey ideas of the Supreme Being. We speak of God as having a heart, and hands, and arms, and feet; of exercising the affections of anger and love, hatred and benevolence, revenge and compassion; in a word, we apply to him most of the expressions used by men, to describe the parts or passions and affections of each other. We are compelled to do so, by the poverty of human language, by the original principles of its formation.

The same holds true, in regard to all descriptions of the invisible world, of heaven and hell. HEAVEN is represented as a *paradise*, i. e. a pleasure garden; as a city with most magnificent walls, structures and ornaments; as a place of perpetual feasting and delight; as a land of rest and overflowing plenty; as a magnificent palace, in which the guests appear adorned with princely robes and splendid crowns, and are admitted to the immediate presence of the great King of kings.

HELL is represented as an abyss; a bottomless pit; a lake that burneth with fire and brimstone, the smoke of which ascendeth up forever and ever; a Gehenna, where the worm dieth not, and the fire is not quenched; as a place of outer darkness, of unceasing and eternal gloom; as a loathsome dungeon, a horrid prison; as a place of torture, and anguish, and unspeakable pain; a place of banishment from God, on which all the vials of

§ 3. *Nature of figurative language.*

his wrath are poured out; and by other such tremendous images, all drawn from natural objects of terror and distress.

That the Scriptures every where pursue this method of representing to us the things of the invisible world, must be familiarly known to every attentive reader of them. That none of these descriptions are to be *literally understood*, seems to be exceedingly obvious; for if any one is to be *literally* understood, *which* is the one? Who will determine this question? If then there are no particular grounds for making any such determination, we must either construe all of them *figuratively*, or all of them *literally*. Not the latter, because then the Bible must be made to contradict itself, beyond all possibility of reconciliation. It must also be made to contradict the nature of the *spiritual* and invisible world. The former, therefore, is the only principle which can be admitted.

The sum of all is, that analogy is brought to the aid of the mind, in such descriptions; which the poverty of language forbade the sacred writers to make out, by any use of words in their *literal sense*. Such a use of them would be, to make the *invisible* world a mere copy of the *visible* one; a world of *spirits* altogether like a world of *matter*. But this cannot, with any show of reason, be charged upon the sacred writers; and therefore we must admit, that the language of which I have been speaking, is employed only in a *qualified, figurative, analogical* sense.

If this principle, so plain, so reasonable, so universally admitted in many cases, be well understood, and thoroughly admitted by my readers in the case before us; we are now prepared, to make a near approach to the question, Whether *Sheol* is ever employed in the *figurative* or *secondary* sense, in the Old Testament?

§ 3. *Nature of figurative language.*

But in order to prepare the way still further, so that we may obtain satisfaction in regard to this subject of inquiry, let us contemplate, for a moment, the use which the Scriptures have made of the words *live* and *life, die* and *death*, in respect to the happiness of the righteous, and the punishment of the wicked.

To live and *to have life* are, beyond all doubt, very often employed in the Scriptures, in order to denote the reward which the righteous shall receive for obedience to the divine commands. Thus Moses says, in the name of God, to the children of Israel, Lev. 18: 5, Ye shall keep my statutes and my judgments; which, if a man do, he shall *live* in them; which is repeated, Neh. 9: 29. Ezek. 20: 11, 13, 21. So Prov. 4: 4, Keep my commandments, and *live;* which is repeated, Prov. 7: 2. Also Is. 53: 3, Hear, and your soul shall *live.* Ezek. 3: 21, If thou warn the righteous man, that the righteous sin not, and he doth not sin, he shall surely *live*, he shall not *die;* repeated in Ezek. 18: 9, 17. 33: 13, 15, 16, 19. Seek ye me, and ye shall *live*, Amos 4: 5, 6.

In the New Testament the instances are very numerous. Luke 10: 28, this do, and thou shalt *live.* John 6: 15, he that eateth me shall *live* by me, [Christ]. John 11: 25, He that believeth, though he were dead, yet shall he *live.* John 14: 19, Because I live, ye shall *live* also. Rom. 8. 13, If ye, through the Spirit, mortify the deeds of the flesh, ye shall *live.* Heb. 10: 28, The just shall *live* by faith. 2 Tim. 2: 11, If we be dead with him [Christ], we shall also live with him. Heb. 12: 9, Shall we not much more be in subjection to the Father of our spirits, and *live?* John 4: 9, He hath sent his Son, that we might *live* through him.

These examples may suffice, in regard to the use of

§ 3. *Nature of figurative language.*

the verb *live*. The noun, *life*, is altogether correspondent with it, in regard to the meanings which it is employed to convey. E. g. Deut. 30: 15, See, I [Moses] have set before thee, this day, *life* and good, and *death* and evil. Here, the words *good* and *evil* are added, merely as explanatory of *life* and *death;* or rather, I may say, they are employed as mere synonymes with them, and serve, by repetition, to give intensity to the affirmation of the speaker, according to the usual custom of the sacred writers. The same expression is repeated, in Deut. 30: 19, with the omission of *good* and *evil;* and manifestly in the same sense as in v. 15. So Jer. 21: 8, I set before you the way of life, and the way of death. Deut. 32: 47, For it is not a vain thing, because it is your *life*. Ps. 16: 11, Thou wilt shew me the path of *life*. Prov. 2: 19, neither take they hold of the paths of *life*. Prov. 3: 18, She is a tree of *life*, to them that lay hold upon her. Prov. 4: 22, They [the words of God] are *life* unto those that find them. Prov. 4: 23, Keep thy heart with all diligence, for out of it are the issues of *life*. Prov. 5: 6, Lest thou shouldest ponder the paths of *life*, her ways are moveable. Prov. 8: 35, Whoso findeth me, findeth *life*. To the same purpose, are Prov. 10: 11, 17. 11: 30. 12: 28. 13: 12, 14. 14: 27. 15: 4. 16: 22. 18: 21. 21: 21. Ezek. 33: 15. Mal. 2: 5.

In the New Testament the instances are very numerous. E. g. Matt. 18: 8 and Mark 9: 43, It is better for thee to enter into *life*, halt or maimed, etc. So 18: 9 and Mark 9: 45, It is better to enter into *life*, with one eye, etc. Matt. 19: 17, If thou wilt enter into *life*, keep the commandments. John 1: 4, In him [Christ] was *life*. John 3: 36, He that believeth not the Son shall not see *life*. John 5: 29, the resurrection of *life*. John 5:

§ 3. *Nature of figurative language.* 101

40, ye will not come unto me, that ye might have *life*. In the like sense, John 6: 33, 35, 48, 51, 53, 63. 8: 12. 11: 25. 14: 6. 20: 31. Acts 3: 15. Rom. 5: 17, 18. 8: 2, 6, 10. 2 Cor. 2: 16. 3: 6. 4: 10, 12. 5: 4. Gal. 3: 21. Phil. 2: 16. Col. 3: 4. 2 Tim. 1: 1, 10. James 1: 12. 1 Pet. 3: 7. 2 Pet. 1: 3. 1 John 1: 1, 2. 5: 12, 16. Rev. 2: 7, 10. 21: 6. 22: 1, 14, 17.

Such are the examples of the method, in which the words *live* and *life* are employed in the Scriptures. That they designate the reward of the righteous, whether in time or eternity, is a clear case; so clear, that I deem all further effort to establish the point, entirely needless. The examples themselves are the most powerful argument which can be adduced.

On the other hand, it is equally plain and certain, that the words DIE and DEATH are employed, in order to designate the punishment of the wicked. From the very numerous examples of this kind, I would present the following; viz.

Ezek. 18: 4, The soul that sinneth shall DIE; which is repeated in 18: 20. So also, in Ezek. 18: 17, he shall not *die*; v. 18, he shall *die*; v. 21, he shall not *die*; v. 21, Have I any pleasure at all that the wicked should *die?* v. 24, In his trespass that he hath trespassed, . . . shall he *die*; v. 26, in his iniquity that he hath done shall he *die*; v. 28, he that turneth away from his transgression . . . . shall not *die*; v. 32, I have no pleasure in the death of him that *dieth.* Prov. 15: 10, he that hateth reproof shall *die.* Prov. 19: 16, He that despiseth my ways shall *die.* Ezek. 33: 8, the wicked man shall *die* in his iniquity; so also in v. 9. In 33: 11, Why will ye *die*, O house of Israel; v. 13 he that hath committed iniquity shall *die;* v. 14, when I say unto the wicked, Thou shalt surely *die;* v. 15, if the wicked . . . walk in the statutes of life . . . . he shall not *die.* Prov. 23: 13, If thou beatest him with a rod, he shall not *die.*

The instance of threatening in Gen. 2: 17, In the day thou eatest thereof, thou shalt *surely die,* (and the like expression in Gen. 3: 3, 4), is to be construed according to the evident tenor of the above examples.

In the New Testament, the usage is exceedingly plain, in various examples; e. g. John 5: 60, This is the bread that cometh down from heaven, that a man may eat thereof and not *die.* Rom. 8: 31, If ye live after the flesh, ye shall *die.* John 8: 21, ye shall seek me, and shall *die* in your sins.

In the like manner is the word DEATH employed, in order to designate the evils consequent upon the commission of sin; e. g. Deut. 30: 15, See, I have set before you, this day, life and good, *death* and evil; in Jer. 21: 8, I have set before you the way of life, and the way of *death.* Prov. 5: 5, Her feet go down to *death.* Prov. 8: 36, All they that hate me love *death.* Prov. 12: 28, In the path-ways thereof, there is no *death.* Ezek. 18: 32, I have no pleasure in the *death* of the wicked; so also in 33: 11.

In the New Testament this usage is very prominent; e. g. John 8: 51, If a man keep my saying, he shall never see *death.* Rom. 6: 23, The wages of sin is *death.* Rom. 6: 21, The end of those things is *death.* Rom. 6: 16, Whether [ye are the servants] of sin unto *death.* Rom. 7: 5, The motions of sin did work to bring forth fruit unto *death.* Rom. 7: 10, The commandment to life, I found to be unto *death.* Rom. 7: 13, Was then that which was good, made *death* unto me? Rom. 7: 24, Who shall deliver me from the body of this *death?*

§ 3. *Nature of figurative language.* 103

Rom. 8: 2, The law of the Spirit of life . . . . hath freed me from the law of sin and *death.* Rom. 8: 6, To be carnally minded is *death.* 2 Cor. 2: 16, To the one we are the savour of death unto *death ;* i. e. a deadly savour causing spiritual death. 2 Cor. 7: 10, The sorrow of the world worketh *death.* 2 Tim. 1: 10, Our Saviour Jesus Christ, who hath abolished *death.* Heb. 2: 14, That through death he might destroy him that had the power of *death.* James 1: 15, Sin, when finished, bringeth forth *death.* 1 John 3: 14, He that loveth not his brother, abideth in *death.* Rev. 2: 11, He that overcometh, shall not be hurt of the *second death.* Rev. 20: 6, On them he *second death* had no power. Rev. 20: 14, This is the *second death.*

The importance of the principle of interpretation, which is connected with examples of this nature, is my apology for producing them at such length. When the mind once becomes entirely satisfied, that the objects of the invisible world can be revealed to us only in language which is already formed, and formed from the notices which our senses, external or internal, take of the objects within their reach; it is then that we begin to have some due apprehension of the nature and extent of figurative language, as employed by the sacred writers. These writers had a vivid impression of the joys of heaven and the pains of hell, of the reward of virtue and the punishment of vice, in the world to come. These ideas they could not convey, in language which originated from notice of these objects taken by any of our senses; there was no such language for their use. They must, then, from the nature of the case, employ such language as they had; they could not use such as they had not, nor such as would be unintelligible to others. Of course,

§ 3. *Nature of figurative language.*

they must employ language, which was originally designed to convey ideas of impressions received by our external or internal senses; and consequently, language designating ideas of sensible objects, in its *primary* and *literal* acceptation.

If now we make the inquiry, why *live* and *life*, *die* and *death*, should be employed to represent the joys and sufferings of the world to come, the answer will not be difficult. *Life* is of all things most dear. "All that a man hath, will he give for his life." *Death*, of course, is of all things most dreaded. It is the consummation of all suffering; the highest penalty which can be inflicted.

Should one, then, range the whole compass of human language, he could find no two terms so significant as these, in order to designate the joys of heaven or the pains of hell. To do this, they must indeed be *figuratively* employed. But the same is true of all other words, that are or could be employed for the same purpose. Of course this is no objection to the use of them.

It is easy to see, therefore, why the sacred writers have chosen these highly significant words, in order to convey an idea of the impression made on their own minds, respecting the joys of heaven and the pains of hell. "The wages of sin is *death*, but the gift of God eternal *life*." Is it in the power of language to convey a stronger impression of the retributions that will be made in the invisible world, than such an expression conveys?

§ 4. *Secondary signification of Sheol.*

If the mind is satisfied in regard to the view of the subject given above, there remains but little to be said,

§ 4. *Secondary signification of* שְׁאוֹל.

in order to satisfy it respecting the possibility of applying *Sheol* (שְׁאוֹל) in a similar way. *Sheol* and *death* are most intimately connected. They often stand together in the same verse, constituting the corresponding parts of a parallelism. Whatever may be said of *death*, as an image of terror and distress, may be applied with equal force to *Sheol*. The *grave, the under-world, the region of the dead*, is of course most intimately connected with *death* itself.

Sheol then may be used in a *secondary* sense, to denote *the world of misery*, the region of " the second death." It is no objection to this, that it is generally employed in its first and literal sense; for such is the case with the words *live, life, die, death*. Yet this does not at all prove, that these latter words are never employed in any other than the literal sense. Such a principle indeed, if admitted, would prove that no words are, or can be, employed in a *figurative* sense; for, in a majority of cases, nearly all words have a *literal* sense.

Suppose now that I should say, The word *God* sometimes means *a carved piece of wood, a molten image,* or *an object of the natural world;* and because it *sometimes* means *a block of wood,* therefore it can never designate the *true God?* Would this reasoning be regarded by any candid and intelligent man as of any validity? Surely not. Suppose then I should aver, that because *Sheol* usually means *grave, sepulchre, under-world,* therefore it never can mean *the world of woe;* would this reasoning be any more conclusive? Plainly not.

If then the words *to die* and *death,* are often employed to designate the misery of the wicked, may we not expect that *Sheol* will partake, with them, of this same usage?

§ 4. *Secondary signification of* שְׁאוֹל.

It will not be said, I trust, that such an expectation is unreasonable or unnatural.

We have seen, then, that there is nothing which can determine, *a priori*, against such a use of the word *Sheol* as has been just described. We may now come, therefore, to examine the question of fact itself, viz. *whether the word is actually so employed*, without being prejudiced against any of the proofs or evidences which may be proffered, in order to shew that such is probably the case.

II. *The cases in which* SHEOL *may designate the future world of woe, I shall now subjoin.*

Job 21: 13, They [the wicked] spend their days in wealth, and in a moment go down to *Sheol*.

Ps. 9: 17 (18), The wicked shall be turned into *Sheol*, and all the nations that forget God.

Prov. 5: 5, Her feet go down to death, her steps take hold on *Sheol*.

Prov. 9: 18, But he knoweth not that the ghosts are there, and that her guests are in the depths of *Sheol*.

Prov. 23: 14, Thou shalt beat him with a rod, and shalt deliver his soul from *Sheol*.

I might add some other texts apparently of the same tenor with these, but I shall defer the mention of them until I have made some remarks on those already produced. My great object is not to multiply the *number* of texts, which may possibly be brought within the limits of such a meaning as I here suppose *Shoel* to have ; but to illustrate the principle, that is concerned with the exegesis of texts which exhibit the word *Sheol*.

In attentively considering the texts just adduced, is it not plain, that the exegesis would be an easy and na-

§ 4. *Secondary signification of* שְׁאוֹל.

tural one, to apply them to *the future punishment* of the wicked? I do not say *eternal* punishment here, because, if we admit that *Sheol* here designates *future punishment*, we must also admit, that it does not determine, of itself, the *duration* of that punishment. After what has been said above, of the Scriptural use of the words. *die* and *death*, it cannot be said, with any show of reason, that it would be strange or singular, that *Sheol* should here designate future punishment; I mean, that it cannot seem strange to any one who acknowledges the Scriptures as revealing the doctrine of future punishment in any form whatever. To those who do not acknowledge this, I am not addressing myself. Such have first to be convinced that the Bible is the word of God, before they can be convinced, by any proofs drawn from it, with regard to future punishment. Although they may not know it, or may be unwilling to acknowledge it, yet they are plainly skeptics as to the divine origin and authority of the Scriptures. To say that the Bible is the word of God, and yet to aver that there is no future punishment threatened by it,—is so palpable an exhibition either of ignorance, or of unbelief, or of dishonesty, that an ingenuous man can hardly believe in any professions of respect for the Bible, which such a person may make.

The probability that *Sheol* designates the *future punishment* of the wicked, in the passages just cited, depends perhaps, in a great measure, on the state of knowledge among the Hebrews, with regard to future rewards and punishments. I am well aware, as I have already hinted above, that there are critics who maintain, that the Hebrews had no knowledge or belief of any such doctrine. But as it is now past all doubt, that the ancient Egyptians (of Moses' time) did believe and teach, very

§ 4. *Secondary signification of* שְׁאוֹל.

expressly, the doctrine in question; I am not able to comprehend how Moses, "who was learned in all the wisdom of the Egyptians," should have been ignorant of this doctrine. Nor, as I have already said, can I be persuaded, without strong, yea irrefragable evidence, that the·people of God, among whom were patriarchs and prophets, knew less respecting a future state of rewards and punishment, than their heathen neighbours who were wholly destitute of any special revelation.

We have, then, no good reason to believe, that the ancient Hebrews rejected the doctrine of the soul's immortality, or even doubted of it. The modern Sadducees, indeed, entertained doubts of this nature. But this sect arose only a short time before the commencement of the Christian era; and the peculiar opinions which it maintained, were derived, beyond all reasonable doubt, from skeptical Greek philosophers. The Pharisees held fast to the doctrines, on this subject, which had been derived by tradition from their ancestors.

Circumstances being such, then, as these considerations shew them to be, I see not how it can ever be made out, with any good degree of certainty, that the texts in question have no reference to future punishment. I admit, that they are susceptible of another interpretation, i. e. that another interpretation is possible. But this does not reach the point in question. Are they not also susceptible of an interpretation, which would make them to designate the future misery of the wicked? Is not this latter interpretation even more probable than the former? An answer to these questions, will touch the difficulty which the case presents.

The first question has been already answered, by the examples produced, of the manner in which the words

§ 4. *Secondary signification of* שְׁאוֹל. 109

die and *death* are employed, by the sacred writers. In regard to the second question; it may be said, that the example in Job 21: 13 is not altogether so probable as to afford entire satisfaction. Verses 17, 18, 21, 30—33, it may be alleged, seem rather to incline the mind to construe *Sheol* in v. 13 as meaning *grave;* and so our English translators have done.

I have no doubt, that the word *Sheol* in this case does involve the idea of *sudden death* or *dying*, as a calamity. The question however is, whether in the mind of the speaker, in such a case, any thing more was probably contemplated, than the simple fact of sudden *natural death?* The answer to this must of course depend on the fact, whether the speaker believed in any future retribution, any future punishment of the vicious and rewarding of the virtuous. In case he did, (and who will undertake to shew that he did not?) then how can we avoid the apprehension, that he connected with going suddenly and violently down to *Sheol*, the idea of a miserable condition there? How can we *rationally* avoid such an apprehension?

In regard to Prov. 5: 5 and 9: 18, both of which have respect to prostitutes, one may ask, What was there in intercourse with them, which tended to sudden and premature death, any more than existed in every Harem of the East, where polygamy is practiced? The question, at the present day, could be easily answered; as disease, in some of its most awful forms, is the usual concomitant of illicit intercourse of this nature. But this disease, so far as I know, was unknown to the ancient world. The Greeks and Romans seem to have known nothing of it. Heathen nations abroad knew nothing of it, until it was communicated to them by Europeans. There was, then,

110   § 4. *Secondary signification of* שְׁאוֹל.

nothing but excess in the intercourse, which was of the nature in question, which tended to sudden or violent death—an excess as frequently practised in Harems, as among prostitutes.

It is not difficult indeed to see, that a person devoted to illicit intercourse with lewd women, might easily squander his estate and reduce himself to poverty. But in regard to the danger of life itself, no important difference can be made out between this case, and that which exists in Harems filled with wives and concubines.

How then can Prov. 5: 5 and 9: 18 have any *special* significancy, if *Sheol* does not here mean something more than *grave?* Neither sudden death, nor violent death, appears to have been specially attendant upon the practice of illicit intercourse, in ancient times. What then is the significancy of the texts before us, if they do not refer to *future retribution?*

So in Prov. 23: 14, it is certainly clear that the meaning will be a good one, if we suppose *Sheol* here to designate *future punishment.* At the same time it may be admitted, that the other meaning, viz. *sudden* and *violent death* or *premature death*, is a *possible* one ; yet on the whole can we regard it as probable, when the verse preceding declares that correction will save a child from *death?* Is not death here the misery which is consequent upon sin? And if so, then does not *Sheol* in v. 14 mean, *a state of punishment?*

I have spoken of *sudden* and *violent death*, or *premature death*, as being the kind of death threatened to the wicked, whenever the threatening has reference merely to the present world. To suppose that *death* simply, without its being sudden or premature, is threatened in these cases, would be a supposition quite idle, and I had

§ 4. *Secondary signification of* שְׁאוֹל. 111

almost said, ridiculous. Do not the righteous die, as well as the wicked ? Is it not " appointed unto *all* men once to die ?" And is there any distinction here, between the righteous and the wicked ? None ; and of course, to threaten the wicked that they should die simply, would be to threaten them not at all ; for the same threat could, with equal truth, be made against the righteous. To die, then, in the usual manner, is not a special penalty of wickedness ; and therefore the threats of death, directed against particular acts of wickedness, can never be rationally regarded as having reference to any thing but *sudden, premature,* and *violent death.* That " the wicked shall not live out half their days," is an assurance, repeated in many forms and in a great variety of ways, in the Old Testament Scriptures.

In this point of view it is possible, I concede, to interpret all the texts which exhibit *Sheol* as having a reference merely to the *grave;* and therefore it is possible to interpret such ones as Prov. 5: 5. 9: 18 and 23: 14, as designating a death *violent* and *premature,* inflicted by the hand of heaven.

After all, I cannot but feel inclined to believe, that the Hebrew, who employed the word *Sheol* in this way, *did of course unite with this sense of it, the idea of misery consequent upon such premature and violent death.* Happy or miserable, after death, the Hebrews must have supposed every one to be. What then was to be the state of him, whose wickedness was such as to bring sudden and premature death upon him ? Surely it cannot well be supposed, that the Hebrews believed such an one would be happy after death.

When I say that the Hebrews believed men would be happy or miserable after death, I do not mean to aver,

§ 4. *Secondary signification of* שְׁאוֹל.

that they had those distinct and definite notions on this subject, which we of the present day have. We should never forget, that it is the glorious preëminence of the gospel, to have "brought life and immortality to light." Christians too often forget this, while reasoning from the Old Testament. But then, to suppose that the Jews had no idea of a future state of retribution, is to suppose them to be destitute of the very first principles of even natural religion; for "he who cometh unto God, must believe that he is, and that he is the rewarder of those that diligently seek him."

On the whole, the balance seems decidedly to be in favour of the idea, that by usage *Sheol*, in some cases, did convey the idea of *future misery*, as connected with the sudden and violent death of the wicked. And this idea may be connected with a considerable number of passages, among the examples adduced under the *first* head above.

The meaning of *Sheol* which lies upon the face of the sacred record, (if I may thus speak), is indeed that of *grave, sepulchre, under-world;* as I have given it in the general recension of the passages. But that the Hebrew might connect, nay, that he probably did connect, the idea of *consequential misery*, with that of violent, sudden, and premature death, cannot be rendered improbable.

Indeed it is very difficult to render it improbable, when we add to the texts above cited, viz. Job 21: 13. Ps. 9: 17 (18). Prov. 5: 5. 9: 18. 23: 14, others which seem to be of the like nature; e. g.

Prov. 7: 27, Her house is the way to *Sheol*, going down to the chambers of death ; comp. Prov. 5: 5. 9: 18.

Prov. 15: 24, The way of life is above, לְמַעְלָה , to the

§ 4. *Secondary signification of* שְׁאוֹל. 113

wise, that he may depart *from Sheol*, מִשְּׁאוֹל , beneath. The most natural meaning of this is ; ' The way of life is that which conducts to happiness above, where God dwells ; and by pursuing this, one escapes *Sheol* or the world of misery beneath.'

Let any one now, in addition to these texts, carefully inspect such passages as Num. 16: 30. 16: 33. Deut. 32: 22, 1 Kings 2: 6. 2: 9. Ps. 49: 14, 15. Is. 5: 14, and then say, whether the Hebrew, believing in a state of future retribution, did not connect such language, in his own thoughts, with the apprehension of future misery in regard to those of whom he thus spake.

I am indeed far from coinciding with those, who find the nature of a future world as *fully* and *plainly* revealed in the Old Testament as in the New. But I am equally far from those, who do not find it at all intimated there. Both these positions are *extremes;* and as such, they should be avoided by every considerate inquirer.

On the whole, it is to be regretted that our English translation has given occasion to the remarks, that those who made it have intended to impose on their readers, in any case, a sense different from that of the original Hebrew. The inconstancy with which they have rendered the word *Sheol*, even in cases of the same nature, must obviously afford some apparent ground for this objection against their version of it. But I cannot persuade myself, that men of so much integrity as the translators plainly were, and, I may add, of so much critical skill and acumen also, would undertake to mislead their readers in any point, where it is so easy to make corrections. I am much more inclined to believe, that in their day the word *hell* had not acquired, so exclusively as at present, the meaning of *world of future misery*. There is plain evidence

11

114   § 4. *Secondary signification of* שְׁאוֹל.

of this, in what is called the Apostles' Creed; which says of Christ, (after his crucifixion), that " he descended into *hell*." Surely the *Protestant* English church did not mean to aver, that the soul of Christ went to the *world of woe;* nor that it went to *Purgatory.* They did not believe either of these doctrines. *Hell* then means, in this document, the *under-world, the world of the dead.* And so it has been construed, by the most intelligent critics of the English church.

With this view of the meaning of the word *hell*, as employed in past times, we may easily account for it, why it has been so often employed as the translation of *Sheol.* This view of the subject, also, enables us to acquit the translators of any collusion in regard to this word ; and to acquit them in this respect, does seem to be an act of simple justice, due to their ability, their integrity, and uprightness.

The sum of the evidence from the Old Testament in regard to Sheol, is, that THE HEBREWS DID PROBABLY, IN SOME CASES, CONNECT WITH THE USE OF THIS WORD, THE IDEA OF MISERY SUBSEQUENT TO THE DEATH OF THE BODY. It seems to me that we can safely believe this; and to aver more than this would be somewhat hazardous, when all the examples of the word are duly considered.

§ 5. *Popular views of Sheol.*

To complete the view of *Sheol* here, I must beg leave to add a few suggestions on the *popular* ideas of the Hebrews, respecting the nature of the *under-world* in general. These may serve to explain some passages of the Old Testament, which, to say the least, must appear

§ 5. *Popular views of* שְׁאוֹל.

somewhat peculiar, unless the *popular* notions respecting *Sheol* are well understood.

The usual method, in which the Hebrews and almost all other ancient nations disposed of the dead bodies of men, was to bury them in the earth. Here they were consumed. From the grave none ever returned to greet their friends among the living; nothing more was ever seen or heard of them.

Still, there has been no nation on earth, so far as we know, certainly no one which had made any considerable advances in cultivation, which has believed that the existence of man entirely terminates with his death. The soul, to which various forms and modes of existence have been assigned, has generally been supposed to survive the body, and to exist in a state peculiar to itself in many respects, and susceptible of various kinds and degrees of joy or of sorrow.

Popular apprehensions in regard to the state of men after death, (and these *only* am I now considering), seem to have been very much affected by the usage of burying corpses in the ground, and by the fact that no more is seen or heard of men after they are thus buried.

The desire of immortality seems to constitute a part of the instinctive affections of the human soul. The belief of immortality is connected intimately with this. But where this belief is cherished, it seems obviously necessary, to assign some place to the soul for existence and action. Where shall this be? How shall they argue and conclude on this subject, who are unenlightened by revelation, or who reason merely from the impulse of imagination, or from the notice of their own senses?

History can answer the question how they have reasoned. The Egyptians, the Greeks, the Romans, and

§ 5. *Popular views of* שְׁאוֹל.

many other nations, have believed in the existence of a *Hades*, of an *Infernus*, i.e. of an under-world, of a region of the dead, in which their departed friends lived and acted. Among each nation, popular superstition or imagination has attached peculiarities of their own to this under-world, or region of the dead; but the general features of it are alike among all.

The *popular* views of the Hebrews appear, in many respects, to have been of the like nature. With them, the *grave* and *Sheol* were often regarded as one and the same, when they designed merely to describe the decease of their friends, and their departure to another world. But at other times, *Sheol* was, as we have seen above, taken in a wider sense than that of *grave* merely; it designated *the world of the dead*, the region of רְפָאִים, i. e. of *umbrae* or *ghosts*. It was considered as a vast and wide domain or region, of which the grave seems to have been as it were only a part, or a kind of entrance way. It appears to have been regarded as extending deep down in the earth, even to its lowest abysses. This was not unnatural. In the present life, men inhabit a region over which the air, שָׁמַיִם, extends indefinitely. Imagination formed something like this, for those who were placed in the sepulchre. A region deep and wide existed all around them. In this boundless region lived, and moved (at times), the Manes of departed friends. To this they assigned many qualities or attributes, some of which will now be briefly noticed.

(1) *Sheol* is a place from which none ever return.

So Job 7: 9, As the cloud is consumed and vanisheth away, so he that goeth down to the grave shall come up no more. He shall return no more to his house, neither shall his place know him any more. –2 Sam. 12: 23,

§ 5. *Popular views of* שְׁאוֹל.

Now he is dead, wherefore should I fast? Can I bring him back again? I shall go to him, but he shall not return to me.

(2) It devours or consumes the bodies laid in it.

Job 24: 19, Drought and heat consume the snow waters; so doth the grave those who have sinned. Ps. 49: 14, Like sheep they are laid in the grave; death shall feed on them .... their beauty shall consume in the grave.

(3) *Sheol* is a place of inaction and silence.

Occasionally this idea is departed from, e. g. Is. 14: 9, and in some other places. The amount of it seems to be, that in general *Sheol* is represented as a place of entire inactivity and silence; e. g.

Ps. 6: 6, In death there is no remembrance of thee; in the grave, who shall give thee thanks? Ps. 31: 17 (18), Let them be silent in the grave. 1 Sam. 2: 9, The wicked shall be silent in darkness. Ps. 115: 17, The dead praise not the Lord; neither any that go down into silence. Is. 38: 18, For the grave cannot praise thee; death cannot celebrate thee. Ecc. 9: 10, For there is no work, nor device, nor knowledge, nor wisdom, in the grave whither thou goest.

(4) *Sheol* extends deep into the recesses of the earth; yea, as deep as the heavens are high above it.

Job 11: 8, It is high as heaven, what canst thou do? Deeper than *Sheol*, what canst thou know? Ezek. 31: 15, Thus saith the Lord God, In the day when he [the king of Egypt] went down to *Sheol*, I caused a mourning, I made the abyss to cover him; i. e. Sheol was below the abyss of the ocean. So Jonah 2: 2. (3), out of the belly of *Shoel* did I cry unto thee; i. e. from the

118   § 5. *Popular views of* שְׁאוֹל.

deep abysses of the sea, (while in the belly of the whale), did I cry unto thee.

Sheol is the common antithesis of שָׁמַיִם, *heaven.* Amos 9: 2, Though they dig into *Sheol*, thence shall my hand take them ; though they climb up to heaven, thence will I bring them down. Deut. 32: 22, A fire is kindled in mine anger, which shall burn to the lowest Sheol. Ps. 139: 8, If I ascend up into heaven, thou art there ; if I make my bed in *Sheol*, behold thou art there.

(5) *Sheol* is a place of utter and perpetual darkness and gloom.

Job 10: 21, 22, Before I go whence I shall not return ; even to the land of darkness and the shadow of death ; a land of darkness, as darkness itself, and of the shadow of death, without any order ; where even the light is darkness ; i. e. where even the day is like our mid-night. The vivid nature of the imagery is very striking.

(6) Here dwell the *ghosts* or *Manes* of deceased men.

Ps. 88: 10 (11), Wilt thou shew wonders to the dead ? Shall the Manes, רְפָאִים, arise and praise thee ? i. e. shall the ghosts from the under-world rise up to life, and praise thee ? Prov. 2: 18, For her house inclineth unto death ; and her paths unto *the ghosts*, רְפָאִים ; i. e. the place where the ghosts dwell. Prov. 9: 18, He knoweth not that the *ghosts*, רְפָאִים, are there ; and that her guests are in the depths of *Sheol.* Prov. 21: 16, The man that wandereth out of the way of understanding, shall remain in the congregation of *ghosts*, רְפָאִים . Is. 14: 9, *Sheol* from beneath is moved, to meet thee at thy coming ; it stirreth up *the ghosts* for thee, רְפָאִים לָךְ .

That רְפָאִים designates *deceased persons,* is perfectly clear, not only from the texts just cited, but from the following passages : viz. Is. 26: 14, They are dead, they

§ 5. *Popular views of* שְׁאוֹל.

shall not live, they are *ghosts, Manes*, [i. e. in a state of decease, having a *post mortem* existence], they shall not rise. Is. 26: 19, Thy dead men shall live ; .... the earth shall cast out her *ghosts*, רְפָאִים.

The *state* of the *Manes* is strongly characterized by the Hebrew name given to them, viz. רְפָאִים, the plural of רָפָא=רָפָה, which means *weak, feeble, powerless* ; an idea almost of course connected with the impression which the mind receives, from examining the powerless state of dead bodies. Accordingly, in Is. 14: 10, the ghosts of *Sheol* are represented as saying to the King of Babylon, as he comes down to them, "Art thou too *become weak* (חֻלֵּיתָ) like us?"

These passages shew, very clearly, a strong resemblance in the *popular* ideas of *Sheol* among the Hebrews, to those of the Greeks and Romans in regard to *Hades*.

(7) *Sheol* is sometimes *personified*, and represented as an insatiable monster, always devouring without remorse or distinction ; e. g.

Is. 5: 14, Therefore *Sheol* hath enlarged herself, and opened wide her mouth without measure. Prov. 27: 20, *Sheol* and destruction are never satisfied. Prov. 30: 15, 16, Three things are never satisfied .... *Sheol*, the barren womb, etc. Prov. 1: 12, Let us swallow them up alive, like *Sheol*.

(8) *Sheol*, in common and popular language, is the world or region to which both the righteous and the wicked go after death.

Thus Abraham was *gathered to his people*, Gen. 25: 8 ; so also was Isaac, Gen. 35: 29 ; Jacob, Gen. 49: 29 ; Aaron, Num. 20: 26 ; Moses, Deut. 32: 50. The generation contemporary with Joshua, were *gathered to their fathers*, Judg. 2: 10.

120 § 6. *Remarks on the popular views of* שְׁאוֹל.

In Gen. 37: 35, Jacob is represented as saying, "I will go down to *Sheol*, unto my son, mourning." David often prays to be delivered from *Sheol;* and often describes the wicked as being sent to Sheol. The passages have all been repeated above; and are too plain to need repetition here.

I might add some other minute particulars, respecting the popular modes of representing *Sheol* or the region of the dead; but these embrace the most important. On these I shall now subjoin a few remarks.

§ 6. *Remarks on the popular views of Sheol.*

First; the *popular* representations of this nature, to which reference is so frequently made in Scriptures, are not the proper ground of estimating the knowledge or belief of enlightened Hebrews respecting a future state.

It seems sufficiently plain, that as the Hebrews believed God to be the rewarder of the righteous, and that he would inflict punishment on the wicked, they could not well suppose, that after death all would in every respect share one common lot. So Ps. 17: 15, As for me, I shall behold thy face in righteousness; I shall be satisfied when I awake in thy likeness. Here the Psalmist refers to a distinction, to be made between himself and the *prosperous* wicked who have a full portion in the present world. Consequently the distinction is not in matters of *worldly* good; but in something after the present life. So Ps. 16: 11, In thy presence is fulness of joy; at thy right hand are pleasures forevermore.

If any one should wonder how the representations of *Sheol* above noticed, should be made in the Scriptures; let him well consider the nature of the *popular methods*

§ 6. *Remarks on the popular views of* שְׁאוֹל.

of representation so often adopted there. In the Scriptures, the sun is represented as *rising* and *setting;* as are also the moon and stars. The earth is an extended plain. The heavens are a solid arch extended over the earth, embosoming the stores of water which supply the rain, and pouring down this through the windows in the vault above. All these and very many other things are represented *simply as they present themselves to the eye.* The sacred writers did not undertake to teach geography or astronomy. Whenever they have occasion to refer to any objects of this nature, they do it merely in the popular way.

Suppose now that any one should undertake, on this account, to maintain that the earth is not a globe, and to deny the revolutions of it, or of the heavenly bodies; and all this, on the authority of Scripture? The times have been, we know, when this was done; but we trust such times are passed away, no more to return.

In the same manner would I reason, in regard to the popular representations of *Sheol* in the Bible. Many of these are strictly correct; as any one may see, by reviewing the particulars above described. But others have no foundation in point of fact. A deep region beneath, peopled with ghosts, is what we do not believe in.

Nor is there any more certainty that it is true, because this method of speaking about it in the Scriptures is adopted, than that the sun goes round the earth, because they speak of it as doing so.

In most cases, it is the language of poetry which employs the popular methods of representation. It is poetry which gives a kind of life and animation to the inhabitants of the under-world. Poetry personifies that world. So in Is. 5: 14, Prov. 27: 20. 30: 15, 16 and 1: 12.

§ 6. *Remarks on the popular views of* שְׁאוֹל.

Above all is this the case, in that most striking passage in Is. 14: 9—20; in which all commentators are compelled to admit a fictitious or imaginary costume. Here the ghosts rise up from their places of repose, and meet and insult the king of Babylon, and exult over his fall. All is life and animation, when he goes down into the under-world.

Yet who was ever misled by this passage, and induced to regard it as a passage to be *literally* understood? But if this be very plain, then are other passages of a nature in any respect similar, equally plain also. To construe them *literally*, and then to build on them arguments, in order to shew that the Hebrews had no more definite views of a future world or of retribution than the heathen, is greatly to abuse the obvious principles of interpretation.

Secondly; another remark which I cannot forbear to to make is, that to represent the Old Testament as determining the future state, either of the righteous or of the wicked, with the *same clearness* and *fulness* as the New Testament does, savours either of prejudice, or of an imperfect acquaintance with the Jewish sacred Records. Where is the *specific* difference between the future state of the righteous and the wicked, *fully* set forth in the Hebrew Scriptures? Where are the separate abodes in *Sheol* for each, *particularly* described? I know not; nor do I believe any one can inform me.

In the New Testament all is clear. "Life and immortality are brought *to light* by the gospel."

It would be a subject of curious and interesting inquiry here, to pursue the comparison of the *popular* notions of the Hebrews respecting *Sheol*, with those of the Greeks as exhibited in the Odyssey, and those of the

§ 6. *General Conclusion.*

Romans as exhibited in the Æneid. Many striking traits of resemblance could easily be pointed out. But it would lead me too far from my present object, to pursue such a course at length; and I must relinquish it to those, who have more leisure for such an undertaking. In the mean time, it is proper to suggest here, that in the view which is to be taken of *Hades* in the subsequent pages, the general ideas of the Greeks and Romans relative to the *underworld*, must necessarily be laid before the reader.

§ 7. GENERAL CONCLUSION.

As has been already intimated above, this is, that WHILE THE OLD TESTAMENT EMPLOYS SHEOL, IN MOST CASES, TO DESIGNATE THE GRAVE, THE REGION OF THE DEAD, THE PLACE OF DEPARTED SPIRITS, IT EMPLOYS IT ALSO, IN SOME CASES, TO DESIGNATE ALONG WITH THIS IDEA, THE ADJUNCT ONE OF PLACE OF MISERY, PLACE OF PUNISHMENT, REGION OF WOE. In this respect it accords, as we shall hereafter see, fully with the New Testament use of *Hades*.

That neither the place of punishment nor of happiness, after death, is as fully and plainly developed in the Old Testament as in the New, will not be called in question by any candid and intelligent reader of the Bible. But that the people of God, in ancient times, had no ideas of future happiness or misery, and no words by which these ideas were conveyed, can be shewn only when it is proved, that those who enjoyed a revelation from heaven, were more ignorant than their heathen neighbors.

ΑΙΔΗΣ or *ΑΙΔΗΣ*.

§ 1. *Classical sense of the word.*

HOMER employs this word, throughout his poems, as the proper name of Pluto, the imaginary god of the *under-world*, among the Greeks and Romans. Later writers, both in poetry and prose, employ it likewise to designate the *region, place, state*, or *condition of the dead; the world beneath* or *under-world; the grave, death* or *the state of death*. As an example of this last meaning, (the only one about which a classical reader will have any doubt), may be cited the phrases, ᾅδης πόντιος, *death by the sea*, ᾅδης φόνιος, *death by murder*. The phrase εἰς (ἐν) Ἀΐδαο or Ἀΐδου, also εἰς (ἐς) Ἀΐδαο and Ἀΐδου, often occurs; but it is elliptical in the Greek, and stands for ἐν Ἀΐδου οἴκῳ and εἰς Ἀΐδου οἴκον, viz. *the house* or *residence of Pluto*.

In the oldest Greek writers, we find *Hades* distinguished from Erebus and Cimmeria. Cimmeria or Cimmerium, was an imaginary place, near the island of Aeea, which island lay off the western coast of Sicily, and was the fabled abode of Circe and her companions, among whom Ulysses and his friends dwelt for some time on his return from Troy. Homer represents Ulysses as setting out from Aeea, and after *one* day's sail, as arriving at

§ 2. *Meaning of Ἀΐδης.*

Cimmeria, on " the extremity of the fathomless Ocean," Odyss. XI. 13. Here they found regions,

Ἠέρι καὶ νεφέλῃ κεκαλυμμένοι· οὐδέ ποτ᾽ αὐτοὺς
Ἠέλιος φαέθων ἐπιδέρκεται ἀκτίνεσσιν,
Οὔθ᾽ ὅποτ᾽ ἂν στείχῃσι πρὸς οὐρανὸν ἀστερόεντα,
Οὔθ᾽ ὅταν ἂψ ἐπὶ γαῖαν ἀπ᾽ οὐρανόθεν προτράπηται·
Ἀλλ᾽ ἐπὶ νὺξ ὀλοὴ τέταται δειλοῖσι βροτοῖσι·

that is, " Covered with darkness and clouds; nor does the sun shining with his beams ever look upon them, neither when he mounts the starry sky, nor when he retires back from heaven to the earth; but deadly night broods over wretched mortals," Odyss. XI. 16—19.

In this Cimmerian region, (which Pliny places near to the Lucrine Lake and Avernus), Ulysses is represented by the poet, as performing the sacred rites which evoked the Manes of the dead from *Hades*, who appeared before him, and successively conversed with him. Once, indeed, Odyss. XI. 474, Homer seems to represent Ulysses as having gone down into Hades; for the shade of Achilles asks him, " Why hast thou dared to come down into Hades?" But still, the picture in general is such, that we are compelled to understand this, as meaning *the precincts of Hades;* for Proserpine and Pluto are represented as sending the Manes *from* their abode to converse with Ulysses; and Hercules, after conversing with him, is represented as " returning again to the house of Pluto," Odyss. XI. 626.

Between this *embouchure* of Hades, (which seems to have been considered as a deep valley or cavity where no light ever comes, but still on the surface of the earth), there lay another region of more intense gloom and darkness, which the Greeks called Ἔρεβος, (comp. the Hebrew עֶרֶב, *night, darkness*). This was not, as some

§ 2. *Meaning of Ἀΐδης.*

of our lexicons represent it, the abode of departed souls; but was only an intermediate region, under the surface of the earth, and lying between this and Hades, which was placed deeper down. Erebus is only *a place of transition* to Hades, from which Homer expressly distinguishes it, Il. VIII. 368.

Last and lowest of all, was Hades, which is subdivided into the upper and lower. In the upper part are the *Elysian fields*, the abode of the good; and beneath these, i. e. in the deepest dungeon, in the bowels of the earth, is Τάρταρος, the place of punishment for the wicked, answering, in some respects, to the Γέεννα of the Hebrews. Later Greek writers do not always observe the distinctions which are here presented, but frequently confound more or less of them in a good degree; as do also the Latin writers.

Virgil in his Æneid, book VI., has given a vivid picture of Orcus or Hades. It is more adapted, however, to convey the fancies of his poetic imagination, than it is to convey an exact idea of the more ancient and general opinions of the Greeks in respect to Hades. He loses sight in some measure of the views of Homer, and is more intent on making out a *striking* picture, than on giving an *exact* account of tradition.

Such is the classical view of Hades and its precincts. As to the state of the *Manes* or *Umbrae* who dwelt in Hades, it may be represented by a few words.

When the shade of Achilles meets Ulysses, at the mouth of Hades, he addresses him thus; "Noble son of Laertes, wily Ulysses, undaunted! What deeds still greater are you devising in your mind? How is it that you have dared to come down to Hades, where the dead dwell who are incapable of forming any plans, the mere resemblances of busy mortals? Odyss. XI. 472—475.

§ 2. *Meaning of Ἀΐδης.*

The words ἔνθα τε νεκροὶ ἀφραδέες ναίουσι, Cowper has translated,

> .... Where the shadows of the dead,
> Forms without intellect alone reside.

But he has overlooked the antithesis lying in ἀφραδέες, *incapable of forming* or *of devising and executing plans.* The idea thus conveyed, is directly the opposite of what Ulysses was doing, and to which Achilles adverts when he asks, "What deeds still greater are you devising in your mind?" The Manes are affirmed by him to be incapable of devising and executing any thing of this nature.

To men who placed the greatest happiness of life in action, as did the ancient Greeks, this would present a gloomy picture indeed of the state of souls in Hades.

Ulysses in his reply to Achilles, seeks to comfort him by reminding him of his former greatness. To all this, the gloomy chief replies;

> Renown'd Ulysses! think not death a theme
> Of consolation; I had rather live
> The servile hind for hire, and eat the bread
> Of some man scantily himself sustained,
> Than sovereign empire hold o'er all the shades.

Cowper's Odyss. XI. 572—597, Greek Original, XI. 487—490.

To the mind of a Greek, this must be a picture of consummate wretchedness.

The picture which Virgil gives, is not less appalling. He describes the Manes and the entrance to their habitation, as

> .... " umbrae silentes;
> .... loca nocte tacentia late;
> ...... res altâ terrâ et caligine mersas;
> .... primisque in faucibus Orci,
> Luctus et ultrices posuere cubilia Curæ;
> Pallentesque habitant Morbi, tristisque Senectus,

§ 2. Meaning of Ἅιδης.

> Et Metus, et malesuada Fames, ac turpis Egestas,
> Terribiles visu formae ; Letumque, Labosque ;
> Tum consanguineus Leti Sopor, et mala mentis
> Gaudia, mortiferumque adverso in limine Bellum
> Ferrcique Eumenidum thalami, et Discordia demens,
> Vipereum crinem vittis in excruentis."
>
> Æneid, VI. 263—280.

Afterwards (VI. 425 seq.) Virgil describes the progress of Eneas in the region of Hades, in terms which shew what a doleful place he thought it to be. However, when he brings his hero to Elysium, to the *locos laetos, et amoena vireta, sedesque beatas* (V1. 637 seq.), he seems to make something more substantial out of them, than can be found in any of the preceding heathen writers. But it is plainly the *fancy of the poet* which does this, and not the tradition of the Greek and Roman nations.

Hades, then, in the view of the Greeks and Romans, was the *under-world*, the *world of the dead*, a place deep in the earth, dark, cheerless; where every thing was unsubstantial and shadowy. The Manes were neither body nor spirit; but something intermediate, not palpable to any of the senses, except to the sight and hearing ; pursuing the mere shadows of their occupations on earth, and incapable of any plans, enjoyments, or satisfaction, which were substantial. Of the Elysium of Virgil, Homer knows little or nothing; and it is sufficiently plain, that it is principally the offspring of his own imagination.

§ 2. *Sense of Ἅιδης as used by the sacred writers.*

Before the New Testament was written, the translators of the Hebrew Scriptures into Greek, i. e. the Seventy as they are usually called, had made very frequent use of the word ᾅδης, in order to translate שְׁאוֹל. They have done this in no less than 60 *instances*, out of the 63

§ 2. *Meaning of Ἅιδης.*

in which the word שְׁאוֹל is employed in the Hebrew original. Twice they have rendered the same Hebrew word by θάνατος, viz. 2 Sam. 22: 6. Prov. 23: 14; and once by βόθρος, *pit*, Ezek. 32: 19 (21).

That they employ the same word (ᾅδης) in a few other cases, is also true. Once they employ it to translate אַבְנֵי בוֹר, *stones of the pit, tomb, grave*, Is. 14: 19; twice, to translate דּוּמָה, *silence*, viz. Ps. 93: 17. 113: 26; and once, to translate צַלְמָוֶת, *death-shade, umbra mortis*, Job 38: 18.

In Is. 38: 18, יוֹרְדֵי בוֹר, *the descenders into the pit*, is rendered οἱ ἐν ᾅδου. In Prov. 14: 12 and 16: 25, דַּרְכֵי מָוֶת, the *ways of death*, is rendered εἰς πυθμένα ᾅδου, *into the depths of Hades*.

These are all the instances in which it occurs in the Septuagint Version. The sense which these translators affixed to it, is most evidently the same as the Hebrews affixed to the word שְׁאוֹל. For this, I must remit the reader to the preceding dissertation, where it has been amply discussed.

In the Apocrypha, I find the word employed 16 times; and in all cases in a manner that corresponds entirely with the use of שְׁאוֹל.

We are prepared then to expect the like use of ᾅδης in the New Testament. Accordingly, we here find it sometimes employed in almost or quite a *literal* sense, i. e. as meaning *world beneath, under-world;* sometimes in a sense similar to that of *Orcus* or *Infernus*, i. e. the place of departed souls; and sometimes in the sense of *kingdom* or *region of the dead*, like שְׁאוֹל in Is. 14: 9 and other passages.

1. Ἅιδης designates the *under-world, subterranean regions* simply, in opposition to the regions above the earth. E. g.

Matt. 11: 23, Thou, Capernaum, which art exalted ἕως τοῦ οὐρανοῦ, *to heaven*, i. e. very highly, (alluding probably to its site on a lofty hill), shalt be brought down ἕως ᾅδου, *to the under-world*, i. e. very low. I admit that the sense is probably a *spiritual* one here, i. e. that the Saviour means to say, that Capernaum, which had been so greatly exalted in point of privileges and had so signally abused them, should be made a conspicuous monument of punitive justice. But still, the source of the imagery, and the natural and primary explanation of the words, are not affected by this.

Luke 10: 15, the same words, in the same sense.

(2) Ἅιδης signifies, *the region of the dead, the domains of death*, or of [him who hath the power of death] Satan.

Thus Matt. 16: 18, Peter is called a rock; and on this rock the church is to be built; " *καὶ πύλαι ᾅδου, and the gates of Hades* shall not prevail against it." The world of the dead was supposed, both by the Hebrews and Greeks, to have bars or gates which none could open, i. e. which were strong or invincible. The reason or ground of this figure, was, that no one ever returned from שְׁאוֹל or ᾅδης, who once went there. The phrase πύλαι ᾅδου may be found in 3 Macc. 5: 51; and πύλαι θανάτου, שַׁעֲרֵי מָוֶת, in Ps. 9: 13. 107: 18. Is. 38: 10. The heathen writers also employ the like phrase; e. g. Euripides, Alcest. 124; Æschylus, Agamemn. 1300; Lucretius, III. 7. These gates, moreover, are represent-

§ 2. *Meaning of Ἅιδης.*

ed by them as most firm and well guarded, Iliad, IX. 312. Odyss. XI. 276 ; comp. Job 38: 17.

The meaning of the phrase in question, then, seems to be ; ' the empire of death shall never prevail over the church,' i. e. the church shall never cease or be extinguished. That *gates of Hades* stands, by synecdoche, for *the region* or *empire of Hades*, is only a common case of rhetorical usage. Strong and invincible as Hades is, it is not to prevail over the church. This will ever live and flourish ; or, it will never die.

As an illustration of the idea of *strength*, to which allusion is made in the word Hades, one may quote the noted line in Petronius, Sat. 62,

" Ecce autem miles, fortis tanquam Orcus."

In the Apocalypse, the imagery is more specific with regard to Hades. The writer of this book not only represents Hades as *the region* or *kingdom of the dead*, but also represents *Death*, θάνατος, as being *king* over this region, and directing and controlling those who dwell in it. Of this tenor are all the examples of the use of ᾅδης in this book ; e. g.

Rev. 1: 18, I have the keys of *death and Hades, τοῦ θανάτου καὶ τοῦ ᾅδου.* The meaning of this is rendered plain, by the context which immediately precedes. The Saviour says, " I live, but was dead ; yea, behold ! I live forever and ever ; for I have the keys of death and Hades ;" i. e. mine is the power to unlock the gates of Hades, to open the doors of this prison from which none could escape. I have entered the region of Hades, (comp. Acts 2: 17, 31), and am come forth living ; yea, in possession of everlasting life.

When God addresses Job, and asks, " Have the gates of death been opened to thee ? Job 38: 17, the question implies the utter impossibility that any merely mortal power should open them. And when Jesus is represented as "having the keys of death and Hades," he is, of course, presented as clothed with power which nothing can control or resist. A special reference, however, is made in this language, to the fact that Jesus had died and risen again; as he says in John 10: 18, "I have power to lay down my life, and I have power to resume it."

Death, which in this passage is tacitly represented as the monarch of Hades, is fully exhibited as such, in other passages of the Apocalypse; e. g.

Rev. 6: 8, Lo! a pale horse, and he who sat upon him was named *Death*, and *Hades followed after him.* Here is the king of the empire of the dead, with his subjects in his train. They are a part of the fearful battle-array which the opening of the seven seals summons together, and puts in readiness to fight "the great battle of God Almighty." Hades, in this passage, stands for the inhabitants of Hades; just as in innumerable cases, we employ the name of a country in order to designate the inhabitants of the same.

It would be turning aside from my present purpose, to descant on the magnificent and appalling scenery presented in Rev. VII. If any one can read this chapter, without being deeply impressed and affected with the vivid and powerful imagination of the writer, he is a very unfit person to be a commentator on this book.

Rev. 20: 13, *Death* and *Hades* gave up the dead which were in them; i. e. the king over the region of the dead, and his empire also, gave up the dead who were under his control or within its boundaries. The meaning of the writer is, that *all the dead* were raised to life,

§ 2. *Meaning of Ἅιδης.*

and summoned to appear before the tribunal of the supreme Judge of the universe.

Rev. 20: 14, and *Death and Hades*, were cast into the lake of fire; this is the second death. Here the king of Hades, and Hades itself, i. e. the region or domains of death, are represented as cast into the burning lake. The general judgment being now come, *mortality* having now been brought to a close, the tyrant death, and his domains along with him, are represented as cast into the burning lake, as objects of abhorrence and of indignation. They are no more to exercise any power over the human race.

Such is the representation of Hades in the Apocalypse. It is the genuine שְׁאוֹל of the Hebrews; with the exception, perhaps, that the Hebrew sacred books have no where represented Hades as having a king over it. The passage in Is. 28: 15, is indeed susceptible of being understood so as to accord exactly with the representation in the Apocalypse; " We have made a covenant with Death (מָוֶת); and with Sheol, (שְׁאוֹל, Hades), are we at agreement;" comp. Hos. 13: 14. But the want of support from analogy in the Old Testament, leads me to construe *Sheol* here, as meaning simply *grave* or *region of the dead*, and as being merely a parallelism of *death*, מָוֶת.

---

(3) Very nearly allied to No. 2, and a species of the same genus, is the meaning, *grave, sepulchre, depository of the dead*, which ᾅδης sometimes has.

1 Cor. 15: 55, *O grave!* ᾅδης, where is thy victory? So our common version here; and well enough, because the question which the writer puts, has respect to *the*

§ 2. *Meaning of Ἅιδης.*

resurrection of the dead. Still, if the passage "O death! where is thy sting? O grave! where is thy victory," should be construed in such a manner as θάνατος and ᾅδης are to be construed throughout the Apocalypse, the sense would be perfectly good; e. g. 'King of terrors! where is thy triumph? Empire of the dead! where is thy victory?'

Acts 2: 27, thou wilt not leave my soul [me] in Hades; nor suffer thy Holy One to see corruption; i. e. thou wilt not leave me in *the grave* or *region of the dead*, nor suffer my body to putrify there. See on שְׁאוֹל above, under Ps. 16: 10.

Acts 2: 31, his soul [he] was not left in Hades, nor did his flesh see corruption.

Both these passages have their basis in Ps. 16: 10; and Hades here, evidently has the same sense as שְׁאוֹל there.

---

(4) *Hades* has the sense of *Tartarus*, in one passage, viz. the region of woe or punishment.

Luke 16: 23, *in Hades*, ἐν τῷ ᾅδη he lifted up his eyes, being in torments. That in the heathen Hades was a *Tartarus*, a place of punishment and suffering, is too well known to need illustration and proof on the present occasion. More will be said on this point, when I come to treat of Τάρταρος. That in Hades, שְׁאוֹל, according to the views of the Hebrews, and of Jesus himself, there was *a place of torment*, is put out of all question by the passage now before us.

Taking this to be correct, we may now look back and see, that the remarks made above on the probable meaning of *Sheol* under §§ 3, 4, receive much confirmation, and are rendered very probable, by the passage before us.

§ 3. *Remarks on the use of Hades in the Scriptures.*

These are all the passages in which Hades is employed in the New Testament. From none of these can we gather, that the Jews in our Saviour's time made use of the word Hades as indicating expressly *the abode of the righteous,* as well as of the wicked. The passage in Rev. 20: 13, 14, may appear somewhat dubious, however, in respect to this point; and the passage in 1 Cor. 15: 55, implies a triumph of the righteous, at their resurrection, over Hades; which would seem to imply, that for a time they had been subjected to its dominion. This dominion, however, need not be interpreted as meaning any thing more, than that they have been subjected to mortality, i. e. to death.

It may also be remarked, that as in the Old Testament, *Sheol* is the place to which the righteous go as well as the wicked; and as the Saviour, subsequently to his death, is represented as being in Hades, Ps. 16: 10. Acts 2: 27, 31; so it is not improbable that the general conception of Hades, as meaning *the region of the dead,* comprized both an Elysium and a Tartarus, (to speak in classical language), or a state of happiness and a state of misery.

Such being the case, the question whether those who go to Hades will be happy or miserable there, depends of course on the question, whether they are righteous or wicked, whether they deserve reward or punishment. Admitting that an existence in Hades implies a state which is capable either of happiness or of misery, is admitting, of course, that the sinner *may be* " in torments" while in Hades; and that Dives was in such a state, is made *certain* by Luke 16: 23.

§ 3. *Remarks on Ἅιδης.*

That the Hebrews used the Greek word *Hades*, so as to correspond in general with their *Sheol*, is quite plain from the above investigations. We can no more argue that Hades, as used by them, did *in all respects* mean the same as it did among the Greeks, than we can argue in like manner in regard to the use of the words θεός, ἄγγελος, σωτήρ, δαίμων, διάβολος, οὐρανός, etc. A most important philological consideration ; and one, I may add, which is very often overlooked in the partial and party examinations to which the Scriptures are not unfrequently subjected !

I add one more remark, before closing this topic. Whatever the state of either the righteous or the wicked may be, whilst in Hades, i. e. under the dominion of death, that state will certainly cease, and be exchanged for another, at the general resurrection. So we are most plainly taught, in Rev. 20: 13, 14. The wicked will then be doomed to a *second death*, more dreadful than the first, Rev. 21: 8, 9, comp. Rev. 20: 8, 9, also Rev. 20: 14, 15.

I am entirely unable, then, to perceive how it can be proved that there will be no future punishment, by shewing that Hades means the *grave, the region of the dead,* or *the state of the dead, the empire of death.* This empire is to cease, and another state is to succeed, from which the Scriptures say nothing (at least I am able to find nothing) in regard to deliverance. When it can be shewn, that there is deliverance from "the lake of fire, which is *the second death*," then something will be done to affect the question under consideration. Until then, I see not how we can avoid the conclusion, that " the smoke of future torment will ascend up *forever and ever.*"

ΤΑΡΤΑΡΟΣ.

The name *Tartarus* occurs no where in the Scriptures. But a *denominative* verb, ταρταρόω, which means *to send to Tartarus, to confine in Tartarus, to punish in Tartarus,* occurs in 2 Pet. 2: 4. Here it is said, that " God spared not the angels who sinned, but ταρταρώ-σας, *confining them in Tartarus, he put them in chains of darkness, incarcerated for trial* or *kept for judgment.*

That a place of punishment is here indicated by *Tartarus*, is put beyond all doubt by the context; " he spared not," " *chains* of darkness," " imprisoned for judgment or condemnation." It remains only to inquire, whether the word is susceptible of any other meaning, even according to the *usus loquendi* of the classics.

In Greek, the word *Tartarus* is employed to designate a supposed subterranean region, as deep down below the upper part of Hades as the earth is distant from heaven; Passow, Lex. sub voc. Τάρταρος. It is occasionally employed, in the later classic writers, for the *under-world* in general; but in such a connection as to shew, that it is only when writers mean to speak of the whole as a region of gloom, that they call it Tartarus. It is the place where the distinguished objects of Jupiter's vengeance are represented as being confined and tormented. It is placed in opposition to, or in distinction from Elysium.

These meanings of the word are so notorious, and so familiar to every reader of the classics, that I deem it unimportant to dwell upon them. I add only, that Homer, Iliad IV. 13, uses the expression εἰς τάρταρον ῥίπτω, which is equivalent to ταρταρόω; Josephus, cont. Apion. 2: 33, uses the expression, ἐν ταρτάρῳ δεδημένους. Καταταρταρόω is also employed by Sextus Empir., Hypotyp. III. 24; and by Apollodorus, Biblioth. I. 1, 2.

There can be no doubt, then, either from classical or sacred usage, of the proper meaning of ταρταρώσας. The only question is, to whom does it refer?

The answer must be, 'Primarily to the sinning angels.' So 2 Pet. 2: 4 shews beyond a doubt. But then the nature of the threatening here is such, that it must be intended for *sinful men* as well as *angels*. So v. 3 clearly shews. The whole strain of the argument is; 'If God spared not the angels who sinned, but confined them in Tartarus; neither will he spare sinners now, but will confine them there.' If we compare vs. 3, 4 and 17, in chap. II., this conclusion is put beyond any reasonable doubt.

I remark, moreover, that the heathen had no apprehension of deliverance from Tartarus. Tantalus, Sisyphus, Ixion, and all others sent there, were doomed to *endless* punishment, in the view of the Greeks and Romans. It remains for those who deny that the idea of such a punishment was attached to the word *Tartarus*, when it was used by the Hebrews, to exhibit some proof that the allegation which they make is true.

But they will tell us, perhaps, that 'the word Tartarus designates nothing more than an *imaginary* place of punishment, among the heathen. Such a place as the Greeks and Romans supposed, does not in fact exist; therefore we are not to conclude, when the word is employed by Peter, that it designates any place which has a real existence.'

The answer to this is easy. We may allow the premises, without in any measure feeling ourselves moved to allow the conclusion. Did not the Greek θεός, designate an *imaginary* god ? Was not his οὐρανός, and his ἠλύσιον (Elysium) *imaginary* ? And yet, when a Hebrew writer employs θεός and οὐρανός, does it designate nothing real, and nothing different from the idea that a heathen Greek expressed by these words ? Surely such an argument as this, can never stand before the light of examination. Have we yet to learn, after so many able lexicons and commentaries on the New Testament Greek have been published, that when the Hebrews employed the words of this language, they attached to very many of them *peculiarities of meaning*, which may be sought for in vain in classic authors ? Who that is worthy of regard as a scholar, now calls this in question ? And if it be true, is there any difficulty in supposing that ταρταρώσας has a *real* meaning, when used by Peter? Certainly none. Indeed, the connection in which it stands, puts this matter beyond fair question. Peter was obliged, when he wrote Greek, to use the language as he found it already made. What term then, in order to express the horrors of future punishment, could he select from the whole Greek language, which was more significant than ταρταρώσας ? Until this question can be answered, I know not how to avoid the conclusion here, that the apostle does refer to a *future* and an *endless punishment*.

ΓEENNA.

THE word Γέεννα is derived, as all agree, from the Hebrew words גֵּיא הִנֹּם; which, in process of time, passing into other languages, assumed diverse forms; e. g. Chaldee גֵּיהִנָּם, Arabic جَهَنَّم (*Gahannam*), Greek Γέεννα.

The valley of Hinnom, גֵּיא הִנֹּם, is a part (the eastern section) of the pleasant Wadi or valley, which bounds Jerusalem on the south, Josh. 15: 8. 18: 6. Here, in ancient times, and under some of the idolatrous kings, the worship of Moloch, the horrid idol-god of the Ammonites, was practiced. To this idol children were offered in sacrifice, 2 K. 23. 10. Ezek. 23: 37, 39. 2 Chron. 28: 3. Lev. 18: 21. 20: 2. If we may credit the Rabbins, the head of the idol was like that of an ox ; while the rest of its body resembled that of a man. It was hollow within ; and being heated by fire, children were laid in its arms and were there literally roasted alive. We cannot wonder, then, at the severe terms in which the worship of Moloch is every where denounced in the Scriptures. Nor can we wonder that the place itself should have been called Tophet, תֹּפֶת, i. e. *abomination, detestation*, (from תּוּף *to vomit with loathing*), Jer. 31: 32. 19: 6. 2 K. 23: 10. Ezek. 23: 37, 39.

Meaning of Γέεννα. 141

After these sacrifices had ceased, the place was desecrated, and made one of loathing and horror. The pious king Josiah caused it to be polluted, 2 K. 23: 10, i. e. he caused to be carried there the filth of the city of Jerusalem. It would seem that the custom of desecrating this place, thus happily begun, was continued in after ages down to the period when our Saviour was on earth. Perpetual fires were kept up, in order to consume the offal which was deposited there. And as the same offal would breed worms, (for so all putrefying meat of course does), hence came the expression, "Where the worm dieth not, and the fire is not quenched."

It is admitted, that the Jews of later date used the word *Gehenna* to denote *Tartarus*, i. e. the place of infernal punishment. The question here to be discussed is, whether this name is *literally* employed in the New Testament, or whether it designates *a place of future punishment* or the future world of woe.

It is of some importance to this investigation, to inquire whether the Jews were ever accustomed to execute malefactors by *burning* them.

That such a mode of punishment was once practiced, and in certain cases even enjoined by the Mosaic law, is certain from Gen. 38: 24. Lev. 20: 14. 21: 9. Josh. 15: 25. But that the Jews were accustomed to execute criminals in this way, in our Saviour's time, there is no certain proof. The allusion, however, in Matt. 5: 22, seems almost necessarily to imply that such was the fact.

The word Γέεννα, then, when used in respect to a place of punishment, may be used, or might have been used, *literally*. The question whether it is employed in its *literal*, or in its *secondary* and *spiritual* sense, in the New Testament, comes now to be examined.

The only passage which seems to me even capable of the *literal* sense, is Matt. 5: 22. The Saviour here says, "Every one who is angry at his brother, is obnoxious τῇ κρίσει," i. e. as it were, to a punishment inflicted by a lower court, viz. that of the *Septemviri* among the Hebrews; "but whoever shall say to his brother, Raca, shall be obnoxious συνεδρίῳ," i. e. to the Sanhedrim (סַנְהֶדְרִין) or highest council, who could inflict severer punishment than the court of Septemviri, q. d. he will deserve still severer punishment than he who is merely angry; "but he who shall say, μωρέ, shall be obnoxious εἰς τὴν Γέενναν τοῦ πυρός," i. e. lit. *to the fire of the valley of Hinnom*, q. d. to a still higher and more severe punishment, such as is inflicted by burning to death in the valley of Hinnom.

Is all this *literal*, or *spiritual?* How can it be *literal?* Our Saviour had just said, that the Jews adjudged him only to be guilty of murder, who *actually killed* a man. He then declares, that in the sight of God, this whole matter appears in a very different light. It is not the *external act* only, which he regards. The *spirit* which is cherished and exhibited, constitutes an essential part of the crime, as it is viewed by him. Accordingly, he who cherishes an angry and revengeful spirit, is exposed to punishment; he who lets this spirit break out into provoking and reproachful language, is more guilty still; but he who gives loose to his passion, so as to utter epithets of the highest reproach, such as would destroy the character or endanger the life of the person against whom they were uttered,—he should be deemed worthy of the most signal punishment of all, like that inflicted in the valley of Hinnom.

It must be very plain, now, to every considerate reader, that the Saviour, (who had just declared that the

Jews regarded nothing to be *killing* or *murder* except the *external* act, and who of course did not punish any thing else or take any cognizance of it), could not here mean to say, that the Jews would *literally* punish the various gradations of crime which he marks. This would be to contradict what he had just said. We must suppose, then, that he means to designate the punishment which God, who could judge the heart, would inflict, and which must be *spiritual*. Surely it cannot be meant, that God would subject persons who cherished anger, to a *literal* court of the Septemviri (*κρίσις*); or to the *literal* Sanhedrim ; or to the *literal* fire in the valley of Hinnom. What is meant must then be, that God would punish, in a future world, with different degrees of severity which were signified or symbolized by the punishment inflicted by the Septemviri, by the Sanhedrim, and by being burned in the valley of Hinnom. It seems impossible to give the passage any other rational, defensible meaning.

It follows, of course, that although Gehenna is here referred to in its literal sense, yet the meaning of the whole passage does not permit us to understand the idea intended to be conveyed as a literal one. It is employed as a source of imagery, to describe the punishment of a future world, which the Judge of all hearts and intentions will inflict.

What has now been said will render the other examples of Gehenna that follow, easy to be understood. Thus,

Matt. 5: 29, the Saviour declares that 'he who does not " cut off" an offending member of his body, shall be cast *into Gehenna*.' Most certainly this cannot be understood of a *literal casting into Gehenna ;* for who was to execute such a punishment ? Not the Jewish courts;

for they had no cognizance of the offence which a man's right hand or right eye moved him to commit, i. e. they could not call in question and punish a member of the human body, because it tempted its owner to sin. It must then be a punishment which God would inflict. But was this a *literal* casting into the valley of Hinnom?

It may however be said, that the caution of the Saviour runs thus; ' Avoid all temptation to sin, lest you bring on yourself the terrible punishment of being burned in the valley of Hinnom, in case you give way to any temptation.'

This would be a possible interpretation, provided the crimes in question could be shewn to be of such a nature as were punishable in this manner by the Jewish courts. But as this cannot be done, this exegesis seems to be fairly incapable of admission.

Matt. 5: 30, another example of the same nature as that in 5: 29.

Matt. 18: 9, an instance of the same nature, excepting that the phrase here is γέενναν τοῦ πυρός, *a fiery Gehenna;* which one cannot doubt has the same meaning as *unquenchable fire,* Mark 9: 43, 45, inasmuch as this very phrase is there used to explain γέεννα; the same meaning also as *the lake of fire,* Rev. 20: 14, 15. 21: 8, which is " *the second death,*" Rev. 21: 9.

Mark 9: 43. 9: 45, the like cases with Matt. 5: 29, and where in both instances, τὸ πῦρ τὸ ἄσβεστον, unquenchable fire is added, in order to explain the tremendous nature of the Gehenna in question.

Mark 9: 47, the same as Matt. 18: 9.

(2) There is a second class of cases, where Gehenna appears to be used more simply still, that is with immediate reference to *the world of woe*, or *a state of punishment*. E. g.

Matt. 23: 15, the Scribes and Pharisees are said to compass sea and land, in order to make proselytes; and when this is accomplished, the proselyte becomes "two fold more *a son of Gehenna* than themselves;" i. e. he is doubly deserving of the punishment of hell. Surely the Saviour does not mean to say, that he will suffer double the punishment *literally* to be inflicted on them, in the *literal* valley of Hinnom.

Matt. 23: 30, how can ye [Scribes and Pharisees] escape *the damnation of Gehenna?* κρίσεως τῆς Γεέννης; Does the Saviour mean here to ask, 'How can ye escape being burned alive in the valley of Hinnom? Were they in any danger of this?

James 3: 6, the tongue . . . is set on fire *of Gehenna*, ὑπὸ τῆς Γεέννης. Does James mean to say, that a slanderous boasting tongue is *literally* set on fire by the valley of Hinnom? Or does Gehenna here mean *hell*, which, like the name of a region or country, is used to denote those who dwell in it, viz. malignant spirits?

---

(3) There remain two examples more, which put the question out of all possible doubt in respect to a *literal* construction.

Matt. 10: 28, fear not them who kill the body, but cannot kill the soul; but rather fear him *who can destroy both soul and body in Gehenna.* The body might, indeed, be *literally* burned in the valley of Hinnom; but the *immaterial, immortal* soul—is that to be *literally* burned there?

Luke 12: 5, fear him, who after killing hath power *to cast into Gehenna;* a passage parallel with the one above, and of the same import.

These are all the instances in which the word Gehenna is employed by the sacred writers. It exists not among the Greek classic writers, because it is a mere Hebrew word. No light then can come from that quarter, in order to illustrate its meaning.

That the word Gehenna was *common* among the Jews, is evinced by its frequency in the oldest Rabbinical writings. It was employed by them, as all confess, in order to designate *hell, the infernal region, the world of woe.* In no other sense, can it in any way be made out that it is employed in the New Testament.

Now as all appellations to designate either heaven or hell, must be taken from sensible objects, (see on Sheol, §§ 3, 4), so there is not the least difficulty as to the usage in question. Heaven is called a *paradise*, Luke 23: 43. 2 Cor. 12: 2. Rev. 2: 7; although this word originally means, *park, garden, pleasure garden*, Cant. 4: 13. Neh. 2: 8. Ecc. 2: 5, and is of Persian origin. So *hell* may be called *Gehenna*, although the original sense of the word is only *valley of Hinnom.* What could be a more appropriate term than this, when we consider the horrid cruelties and diabolical rites which had been there performed? Indeed, it seems quite probable, as Gesenius suggests, that 'Gehenna came to be used as a designation of the infernal regions, because the Hebrews supposed that demons dwelt in this valley.' Hebrew Thesaurus, sub. voc. גיא.

GENERAL REMARKS.

AND now, in view of the results which the whole of the preceding investigations afford, what says the understanding? What says conscience?

The question is not, what this or that individual may *wish* or *desire* to be true; but, *What have the sacred writers taught?* This latter question can be answered in no satisfactory way, but by inquiring what the language means, which they have employed. The meaning of this is surely to be made out by *philology*, i. e. by an investigation conducted agreeably to the principles of language; not by *philosophy*, i. e. by *a priori* speculations about the nature of God's moral government. And even in this latter method, if *analogy* is of any force, the question must be decided in the affirmative with regard to future punishment. What earthly government ever existed, or can exist, without any punishments?

Is there, then, a *moral* government of God as a spiritual being? Is there another world, where moral beings are to be governed? If so, who can render it probable, even by *a priori* argument, that there is no punishment there?

But *our* question is with the *Bible.* Does this reveal *a place* of future punishment? To say that this is absurd, or impossible, is only to prejudge the question without examining it. The results of a *philological* examination of the Scriptures, are, that a place of punishment after death is disclosed by the sacred writers, and by the Saviour of men. I am well aware that this is contradicted and denied. But then, neither contradiction nor denial, in this case, springs from *philology*, but from inclination, wishes, philosophy, or prejudice. If this be not so, why is not philology arrayed, in all its proper strength, against the idea that there is a place of future punishment? Who has done this? How is it to be done? All the examples in the Scriptures, of the various words above examined, are produced in these essays. There is no concealment. I trust there is no attempt to pervert or fritter away their obvious meaning. I am certain there is no such design, on my part. Let them be philologically and critically set aside, or shewn to be erroneously interpreted, and, so far as I am concerned, I promise to institute *denovo* another examination.

I address those who acknowledge the Scriptures as the source of their faith; and I put again the questions; What says the understanding? What says conscience?

If any one should reply, and say; 'The words Sheol, Hades, Tartarus, and Gehenna, all have a *literal* signification, and designate objects real or imaginary belonging only to the present world;' the answer to this has already been given. It is simply this, viz. that all words which characterize a future world, are and must be of the like nature. They *all originally* have a *literal* sense. This they must have, else they could not be used in a figurative or secondary sense. The Hebrew שָׁמַיִם, *heavens*, has a literal sense; and so also the Greek *οὐρανός*; both mean *the airy region above the earth, the welkin above,*

General Remarks. 149

the apparent expanse over our heads. But have they, therefore, no other sense ? Do they not often designate the place where God dwells, the abode of the blessed in a future world ? None will be so unreasonable as to deny this.

Paradise, (Heb. פַּרְדֵּס, Greek παράδεισος), has a literal sense, viz. that of *garden, pleasure-garden, orchard of fruit and flower trees*, etc.; but has it *always* such a meaning ? When our Saviour tells the penitent thief, that he should be with him in *paradise;* or when Paul was caught up into *paradise;* or when the Saviour promises to the Ephesian church, that he who overcomes shall eat of the tree of life in the *paradise* of God, is nothing but a *literal garden* meant? The most zealous advocates of benevolence and good-will (so called), would blush at such an interpretation as this.

When the wicked, then, are represented as being sent to *Sheol;* and the rich man as lifting up his eyes in *Hades, being in torments;* or the evil angels as being confined in chains of darkness in *Tartarus;* is all this to be understood only of a *literal* grave, or sepulchre, or under-world ? And when we are commanded to fear him, who can destroy both soul and body in *Gehenna;* is this destruction to be a *literal* one in the *literal* valley of Hinnom ? Prejudice may possibly affirm this; or unbelief may scoff at it, and refuse to examine it; but the reason and conscience of any man, who really believes the divine word, will tremble to decide in so unreasonable and presumptuous a manner.

I advance one step further. There is not only a place of future punishment, (just as surely as there is of future happiness, and on the like grounds), but that place is separated by an "impassable gulf" from the region of the

150 *General Remarks.*

blessed. So the awful passage in Luke 16: 19—26 informs us. The words of this passage, be it remembered, are those of the Saviour, who knows whether there is a hell as well as a heaven. They then that " would pass from the Hades of torments to the region of the blessed, CAN NOT." (Luke 16: 26.) There is no commutation of place for them.

The force of all this may be denied ; attempts may be made to fritter it away ; they have been. There is no difficulty in all this. But how the IMPASSABLE GULF fixed between heaven and hell by an ALMIGHTY GOD, is to be removed, or rendered *passable;* is a question which those who deal thus with the Saviour's words, would do well seriously and timely to consider.

It may be well to notice one more allegation, which has of late been strongly insisted on, and greatly confided in, by many who wish the doctrine to be true which denies that there is any future punishment. In substance it is this ; viz. ' that inasmuch as Hades and Sheol, Tartarus and Gehenna, designate either imaginary regions which are supposed to be subterranean, or else literally the valley of Hinnom at Jerusalem ; it follows of course, that no *real place* of future punishment is named in the Scriptures ; and *if no place is pointed out, then we have reason to conclude that there is none.*'

On this I remark, (1) That the same argument would prove, that since שָׁמַיִם or οὐρανός, and פַּרְדֵּס or παράδεισος, i. e. *heaven* and *paradise,* mean the *region over our heads* and *a garden*, therefore there is no *place* in which the righteous will be happy, unless it be in our atmosphere or in some earthly garden. On this argument I have already said all that I wish to say. " What proves too much, proves nothing."

General Remarks. 151

(2) The laws of our Commonwealth declare, that the man who commits murder shall be punished with death, i. e. with hanging by the neck until death supervene. Now these same laws have no where said, *in what place* the gallows for hanging a murderer shall be erected ; nor even that any shall be erected. Suppose then I deduce from this, the conclusion that a murderer will not be punished, because no *place* for his execution is designated. In reasoning thus, I do just what is done, when conclusions such as I am now examining, are made.

Supposing it to be fact, that the Bible has no where named the *place* in which future punishment will be inflicted ; does this even touch the question, whether there will be any future punishment? An answer to this is altogether superfluous.

But the assumption itself is as ungrounded as the argument. In proof of this, I must refer the reader to the preceding pages. It is labour worse than lost, then, to publish books to prove that there is no future punishment, by such an ungrounded and manifestly erroneous argument as this.

One more remark and I have done, for the present. Let the sober inquirer, who wishes to know the truth, review the meaning of αἰών and αἰώνιος, and ask, whether the probability that future punishment will be *endless*, does not mount so high, that to call it in question is unreasonable and *hazardous ?* And if so, then to believe in the salvation of all men, and to live in such a manner as those usually do who thus believe, is presumptuous beyond the power of human language to express.

If Universalists are in the right, we who believe in a doctrine very different from theirs, are nevertheless just as safe as they. We need not concern ourselves to examine whether we are in the right or in the wrong as to opinion, since there can be no difference in the result. But if we are in the right, and they mistake fundamentally the meaning of God's word ; and mistake it through the spirit of unbelief, and through desire to live without that self-control and self-denial which the gospel demands on penalty of everlasting death ; then what is to be the end of all this ?

Is there any other case, any one that pertains merely to the present world, in which a man of common understanding and prudence, could justify a risk like that in the present case ? And are the interests of *eternity* to be more lightly regarded than those of *time ?* Is the fancied pleasure of the undisturbed gratification of sensual appetites, for a few days, to be put in serious competition with the interests of a period which has no end ? If so, then we may well say with the Scriptures, " Madness is in their hearts while they live, and after that they go to the dead."

But O the *never dying* soul ! The judgement to come ! The summons to appear before that tribunal on which eternal justice is seated ! " Knowing the terrors of the Lord, we would fain persuade men." " It is indeed a fearful thing to fall into the hands of the living God, who is a consuming fire ;" who has said, " Vengeance is mine, I will repay." Blessed are those " over whom the *second death* hath no power !" Dreadful beyond the power of language to describe, beyond what any human mind can possibly conceive, must be the condition of those, who will finally be *cast into the lake of fire, which is the* SECOND *death,* and there be *tormented with the beast and the false prophet, day and night*, FOREVER and EVER.

APPENDIX.

While the preceding sheet was under the press, the Christian Examiner for Sept. 1830 came to hand; which contains a piece occupying 25 pages, dated *Sandwich*, and subscribed E. S. G., making strictures on my remarks (p. 72 seq. of the present edition), which were formerly published in the *Spirit of the Pilgrims* for Aug. 1829. Inasmuch as I have taken the liberty to animadvert on Mr. G's first piece respecting αἰών and αἰώνιος, it would seem to be no more than courteous, to make some answer to his recent suggestions.

The tone and spirit of the whole piece, seem to me to exhibit a singular mixture of courteousness and irritability; now the ἀγαθοδαίμων, and now the κακοδαίμων (I mean no harm) seeming to be uppermost. But on the whole, the former appears to have the mastery; and I am bound to believe him to be rather a good natured man than otherwise; especially considering the provocation that he had, which was no less than the contradicting of his main positions, and the endeavouring to pull down the corner-posts of his building.

I have read with attention Mr. G's vindication, and must confess myself no better satisfied than with his first piece. An examination in detail, my limits do not admit me to make. If Mr. G's main positions are not fast ones, and this can be shewn, I hope he will be satisfied that a minute and extended examination of all the particulars of his piece is required neither by the laws of argument nor of Christian courtesy.

Mr. G. reproves me for saying that the ground of his translating αἰώνιος *spiritual*, is, that *Æons* (Αἰῶνες) were counted as spiritual beings. He admits that he did refer to this, as being ' an *ancient* and *classic* sense of the word ;' but he avers, that he did not rely upon it.

As Mr. G's original piece can be consulted and compared with mine, by those who desire to do so, I will not endeavour to vindicate myself here. I cast myself on the judgement of the reader. He still maintains (p. 26), as he first did, that " αἰών means *spiri-*

tuality, in the more ancient Greek," and that 'the Seventy probably used it in a kindred sense in their version.'

In opposition to this, I shall merely state, that no *classic* Lexicon within the range of my consultation, gives such a sense to the word. Passow's Lexicon, the last and best of all, does not even advert to it. I have never met with it in any classic Greek writer; and consequently I must believe that no such meaning ever was attached to it in ancient Greek, until I see some *evidence* of it; for no evidence has Mr. G. even attempted to offer.

Mr. G. states that his principal reliance is on 1 John 5: 11, 12. 3: 15 etc.; together with some other texts of the like nature, but where the meaning *spiritual*, is rather probable than *necessary*, p. 22. He complains that I have left this unnoticed.

I did so, because I could not conceive how the sentiment in these passages could have a bearing on the question whether αἰώνιος means *spiritual*. The sentiment in both seems to me plainly to be, that a state of happiness and peace (ζωή) begins when the soul is truly reconciled to God, and continues *forever*. As to the first, we may compare John 3: 36, 18. Eph. 1: 12, 13. 4: 30. 2 Cor. 5: 5. 1: 22, comp. Rom. 8: 23, also Rom. 5: 1—11. As to the second, viz. that the *earnest* of future blessedness here given to the children of God, is an earnest of blessedness which will have no end, see Rom. 5: 5—10. 8: 28—39. John 10: 27—30. Yet with all this admitted and taught, as it is, every where in the Bible, the Scriptures make a very wide distinction between the *present* and *future* state of happiness; see Rom. 8: 24, 25. 8: 18—23. 2 Cor. 4: 16—18. 5: 1—5; which are only a specimen of a great multitude of texts of the same tenor.

Now all which the texts relied on by Mr. G. can well be supposed to prove, is, that the happiness in question *would have no end*. There is the same propriety in applying the sense *eternal* here, that there is in all the cases under § 10. No. 1, p. 46 above; which I desire the reader to consult. One might just as well propose to exchange *everlasting* in all these cases for *spiritual*, as to do so here.

It is a sound rule in philology, 'never to depart from the *ordinary* sense of a word, unless the context imperiously demands it.' What there is which *demands* it here, I cannot see. To say that *spiritual* would make good sense, is saying nothing to the purpose. In thousands of cases, where the adjective *good* is applied to God, *almighty* would make good sense; and *vice versâ*. And so of a multitude of other words. But after all the only question is, *What sense did the writer mean to convey?* Not, what may in itself be a good or true sense? Mr. G. must admit this; and admitting it, all which he has said about the word *spiritual* making good sense, falls at once to the ground.

Mr. G's argument on p. 23 seq., has its basis in the *supposed* fact, that the Greek classic language does employ αἰώνιος in the sense of *spiritual*. He tries to shew how the *philosophic* meaning *aeonic*, might become generalized by popular use so as to express *spiritual* simply. But still, αἰώνιος in the sense of *aeonic* and *spiritual*, is an *utter stranger* to classic Greek; the first exists only in the works of some Gnostic heretics, or rather of the *patristic* commentators on them; and of the second, no certain example has yet been offered.

In p. 25 seq. Mr. G. argues, after all, that the principal ground of investigating the true apostolic use of *αἰώνιος*, is the use of it by the Seventy, who regarded it as being correspondent to the Hebrew עֹלָם עוֹלָם (עֹלָם). I accept the terms of contest here proposed, at once, and enter the lists with entire readiness.

All turns now on the Hebrew word עוֹלָם. But this is surely as insecure a basis as Mr. G. could well choose. Among all the Lexicons of the Hebrew language, of which I have any knowledge, (and most of all that have enjoyed much reputation in the Christian world are among this number), I know of none that gives *spirituality* or *spiritual* as the meaning of עוֹלָם. I know of no passage, in the hundreds of places where this word is used in the Old Testament, in which the meaning in question seems in any degree probable.

'But עֹלָם, in Hebrew, means something that is hidden, *mysterious, unsearchable, unknown;*' it is 'well calculated, therefore, to express what is immaterial, intellectual, *spiritual.*'

As to the *mysterious, unsearchable,* or *unknown* in the sense of being beyond the boundaries of knowledge, (which is here implied), I know of no cases in which even the *verb* עָלַם certainly conveys any of these meanings. *To hide, to conceal,* it does mean; but how remote this may be from *mysterious* and *unsearchable,* need not be said.

Then, is there nothing *mysterious* or *unsearchable,* but *spirit?* For example; the powers of nature, gravitation, electricity, magnetism, the principles of vegetation, etc.; is there no נֶעְלָם here?

Once more; even all these meanings belong exclusively to the *verb* עָלַם, and not to the *noun* עוֹלָם. Mr. G. has wholly overlooked this, and therefore committed a radical error in his philological reasoning. He does not need, I trust, to be told, after all which lexicography has done, that nouns derived from verbs, or verbs from nouns, do, by usage, often acquire a sense entirely diverse from what their etymology would indicate. *Usus et jus et norma loquendi.*

But admitting all which he claims, it amounts to nothing; for *hidden* or *mysterious,* can in no way be made *necessarily* to mean *spiritual* or *intellectual.* And even if they could, to argue from what *might be* to what *is,* i. e. from *possibility* to *fact,* would not seem to be very sound philology.

A second argument against his view (exhibited on p. 74 above), is, that it would make *spiritual happiness* or *misery* to begin only *after* the general judgment. In respect to this, Mr. G. avows that I have totally misunderstood him. He says, that "in the article in the *Examiner,* no allusion is intended to be made to any *general* judgment whatever. I do not believe there ever will be any. The assembled universe, so often spoken of as gathered before the throne of God . . . . is, I believe, a mere ' coinage' of the human ' brain.' Certainly the Scriptures assert no such thing," p. 30.

This is coming out very frankly; and I commend Mr. G. for saying what he thinks on this subject. But as to his opinion, viz. that ' the Scriptures assert no such thing as a *general* judgment,' I must merely ask the reader to open his Bible and examine Matt. 7: 22. 25: 31—46. Acts 17: 31. Rom. 2: 5, 6 comp. with 2: 16. John 5: 22, 26—29. 2 Pet, 3: 8—13. Rev. 20: 11—15. I might multiply references of such a nature indefinitely; but these must be sufficient. If these do not establish the fact of a *day* of judgment, and of a *general* judgment, then I must acknowledge myself incapable of interpreting Scripture language.

It is well indeed, that the public should know how far they will be required to go, in order to get rid of the argument to prove that αἰώνιος means *eternal.* I thank the writer in question for telling them this secret.

In regard to the remainder of Mr. G.'s piece, I am entirely willing to let the subject rest where it is. The public have both sides before them, and can judge for themselves.

Why has not Mr. G. once noticed the subject brought to view on p. 62 above? How is he to prove that heaven is *endless*, or that God is *eternal*, if αἰών and αἰώνιος fail to prove it? Can not the like objections be made to any other words, applied to either of these, as to αἰώνιος, viz. that they are susceptible of another meaning?

Mr. G. wishes to know, how I can prove that the *same* means of grace are not used upon sinners in another world, as in this; nay, that more powerful means are not used, p. 43.

My answer is; The *urgency* with which acceptance of the calls of mercy are pressed here; the awful considerations stated in such passages as Prov. 1: 24—28. Matt. 25: 31—46. Heb. 6: 4—6. 10: 26—31. Luke 16: 19—26. Rev. 20: 10—15. 22: 11, 12. Heb. 9: 27; the direct assertions that future punishment is incapable of remission, Mark 9: 43—48 and other like passages; the " everlasting destruction from the presence of the Lord and the glory of his power," 2 Thess. 1: 9; all these are proofs that the *presence* of God is not with the damned, in a gracious sense, and that there is no hope for them. I ask now for one single proof from all the Bible, to contradict this. This I asked before; but Mr. G. has not proffered it.

Mr. G. may conjecture one thing; I have of course the same liberty to conjecture another. Mr. G. may use one argument *a priori*; I, another. But where is the end of all this? Mr. G. well knows that my creed is, THE SCRIPTURES ARE THE SUFFICIENT AND ONLY RULE OF FAITH AND PRACTICE. Whether he admits or rejects this, I know not. But I can never be convinced that he is right in his positions, until I am convinced that the *Bible* vouches for them; and this I cannot ever see in a satisfactory manner, until it is made out in a way compatible with historical facts and philological principles.

www.ingramcontent.com/pod-product-compliance
Lightning Source LLC
Chambersburg PA
CBHW070907160426
43193CB00011B/1391